THE ANCIENT
EGYPTIAN
= WORLD =

STUDENT STUDY GUIDE

Oxford University Press, Inc., publishes works that
further Oxford University's objective of excellence
in research, scholarship, and education.

Oxford   New York
Auckland   Cape Town   Dar es Salaam   Hong Kong   Karachi
Kuala Lumpur   Madrid   Melbourne   Mexico City   Nairobi
New Delhi   Shanghai   Taipei   Toronto

With offices in
Argentina   Austria   Brazil   Chile   Czech Republic   France   Greece
Guatemala   Hungary   Italy   Japan   Poland   Portugal   Singapore
South Korea   Switzerland   Thailand   Turkey   Ukraine   Vietnam

Published by Oxford University Press, Inc.
198 Madison Avenue, New York, NY 10016
www.oup.com

ISBN-13: 978-0-19-522296-8 (California edition)   ISBN-13: 978-0-19-522165-7

Writer: Shelle Sumners
Editor: Robert Weisser
Project Editor: Lelia Mander
Project Director: Jacqueline A. Ball
Education Consultant: Diane L. Brooks, Ed.D.
Design: designlabnyc

Casper Grathwohl, Publisher

Dear Parents and Students:

This study guide has been created to increase student enjoyment and understanding of *The Ancient Egyptian World*. It has been developed to help students access the text. As they do so, they can learn history and the social sciences and improve reading, language arts, and study skills.

The study guide offers a wide variety of interactive exercises to support every chapter. Parents or other family members can participate in activities marked "With a Parent or Partner." Adults can help in other ways, too. One important way is to encourage students to create and use a history journal as they work through the exercises in the guide. The journal can simply be an off-the-shelf notebook or three-ring-binder used only for this purpose. Some students might like to customize their journals with markers, colored paper, drawings, or computer graphics. No matter what it looks like, a journal is a student's very own place to organize thoughts, practice writing, and make notes on important information. It will serve as a personal report of ongoing progress that your child's teacher can evaluate regularly. When completed, it will be a source of satisfaction and accomplishment for your child.

Sincerely,

Casper Grathwohl
Publisher

This book belongs to:

_____

CONTENTS

THE WORLD IN ANCIENT TIMES

The World in Ancient Times *will introduce you to some of the greatest civilizations in history, such as ancient Rome, China, and Egypt. You will read about rulers, generals, and politicians. You will learn about scientists, writers, and artists. The daily lives of these people were far different from your life today.*

The study guides to The World in Ancient Times *will help you as you read the books. They will help you learn and enjoy history while building thinking and writing skills. They will also help you pass important tests and just enjoy learning. The sample pages below show the books' special features. Take a look!*

Before you read

- Have a notebook or extra paper and a pen handy to make a history journal. A dictionary and thesaurus will help you too.

- Read the two-part chapter title and predict what you will learn from the chapter.

- Quotation marks in the margin show the sources of ancient writings. The main primary sources are listed next to the chapter title.

- Study all maps and photos. Read the captions closely. (This caption tells that the statue itself is a primary source. Artifacts are records of history, just like writings.)

" TOMB, SARCOPHAGUS, AND STATUE FROM ROME; AULUS GELLIUS; AND LIVY

CHAPTER 5

FATHERS, GODS, AND GODDESSES
RELIGION IN ANCIENT ROME

Cornelius Scipio Hispanus was not a modest man. He praised not only himself, but his whole family as well. When he died around 135 BCE, the epitaph written on his tomb listed his many elected offices, followed by four lines of poetry, bragging about his accomplishments:

" Tomb from Rome, 133 BCE

By my good conduct, I heaped
honor upon the honor of my family;
I had children, and I tried to equal
the deeds of my father;
I won the praise of my ancestors
and made them glad I was born;
My own virtue has made noble my
family tree.

For generations, the Scipio men had served in high offices. And by the second century BCE, the Scipios had become Rome's leading family. They decorated their family tomb with marble busts of important family members. The oldest sarcophagus contains the body of a Scipio who was a consul of Rome in 298 BCE. Its dedication reads: "Lucius Cornelius Scipio Barbatus, son of Gnaeus, a brave and wise man, whose handsomeness matched his bravery. He was consul, censor, and aedile among you. He captured . . . many cities for Rome and brought home hostages."

" Statue from Rome, 50–25 BCE

" Sarcophagus from Rome, 298 BCE

Like other patricians, Scipio Hispanus proudly claimed his ancestors as founding fathers of Rome. He was probably much like the Roman in this statue. Even though scholars cannot tell us this person's name, we can learn a lot just by

As you read

- Keep a list of questions.

- Note **boldfaced** words in text. They are defined in the margins. —————
  Their *root words* are given in *italics*.

- Look up other unfamiliar words in a dictionary.

- Find important places on the map on pp. 12–13.

- Look up names in Cast of Characters on pp. 8–11 to learn pronunciation.

- Read the sidebars. They contain information to build your understanding.

After you read

- Compare what you have learned with what you thought you would learn before you began the chapter.

looking at him. First: he's a Roman. We know because he's wearing a toga, the garment that was a sign of manhood. The Romans called it the *toga virilis,* and a boy wasn't allowed to wear it until he became a man, usually at 16. Second, because this unknown Roman is carrying masks of his ancestors, we know that his father or grandfather had served as one of Rome's top officials.

These masks, made of wax or clay, usually hung in the hallways of the ancestral home. Romans took them down and carried them in parades and funeral processions.

Roman families were organized like miniature states, with their own religions and governments. The oldest man in the family was called the **paterfamilias,** the patriarch. He was the boss, and his words were law. Scipio Hispanus was the paterfamilias in his family. This meant that he held lifelong power, even over life and death. He could sell or kill a disobedient slave. He had the right to abandon an unwanted baby, leaving him or her outside to die. Usually this would be a sick child or a baby girl to whom the family couldn't afford to give a dowry when she grew up. Romans wanted healthy sons to carry on the family name, yet a father could imprison, whip, disown, or even execute a son who committed a crime. In 63 BCE, a senator named Aulus Fulvius did exactly that after his son took part in a plot to overthrow the government. But this didn't happen very often. Roman fathers were expected to rule their families with justice and mercy, the same way that political leaders were expected to rule the state.

For both the family and the state, religion played a major role in life. Every Roman home had a shrine to the household gods, the Lares. The father served as the family's priest. Scipio Hispanus would have led his family's prayers and made sacrifices to honor their ancestors and please the gods that protected the entire family—living and dead. When a baby was born, Scipio Hispanus would have hit the threshold of his home with an axe and a broom to frighten away any wild spirits that might try to sneak in. When a household member died, family members carried the body out feet first to make sure that its ghost didn't run back inside. (That's why people still sometimes describe death as "going out feet first.")

vir = "man"
Roman boys donned the *toga virilis* when they became men. *Virilis* is a form of *vir;* "virile" means "manly."

pater + *familias* = "father" + "family"
The paterfamilias was the oldest male member of a Roman family.

TOMBS OF THE SCIPIOS

The Romans believed that the dead should neither be buried nor cremated inside the city walls. They were afraid that Rome's sacred places would become polluted by the presence of death. So they lined the roads leading away from Rome with monuments built to house and honor the dead. Visitors can still see the tombs of the Scipios buried along the Appian Way, about two miles from the Forum. (The Appian Way is a military road that was built in the fourth century BCE.)

The next two pages have models of graphic organizers. You will need these to do the activities for each chapter on the pages after that.

Go back to the book as often as you need to.

GRAPHIC ORGANIZERS

As you read and study history, geography, and the social sciences, you'll start to collect a lot of information. Using a graphic organizer is one way to make information clearer and easier to understand. You can choose from different types of organizers, depending on the information.

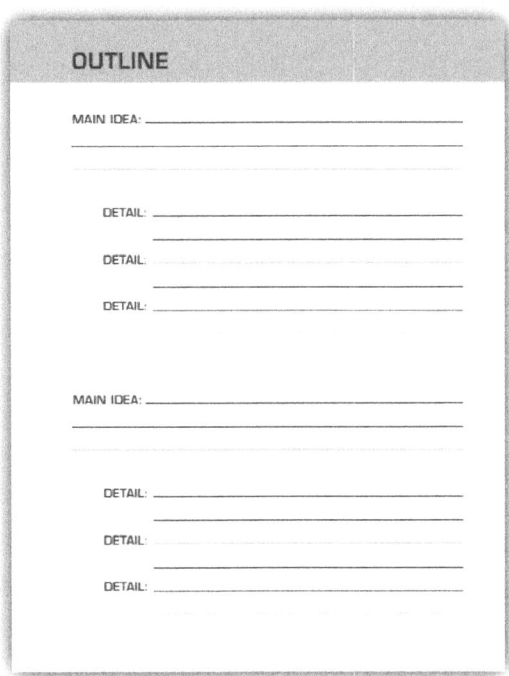

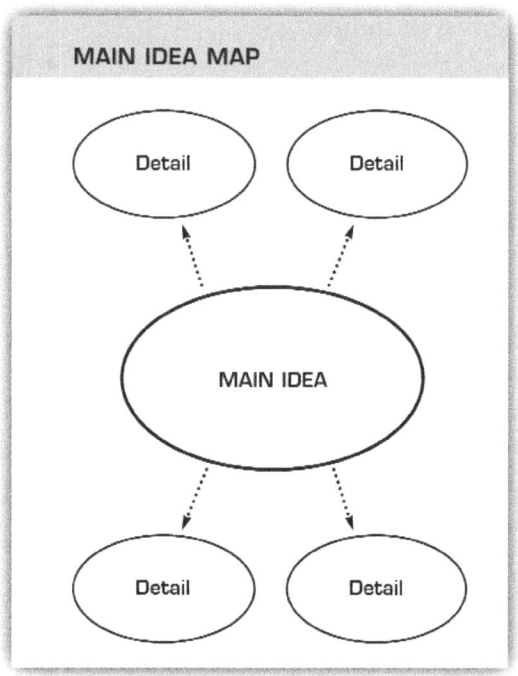

Outline

To build an outline, first identify your main idea. Write this at the top. Then, in the lines below, list the details that support the main idea. Keep adding main ideas and details as you need to.

Main Idea Map

Write down your main idea in the central circle. Write details in the connecting circles.

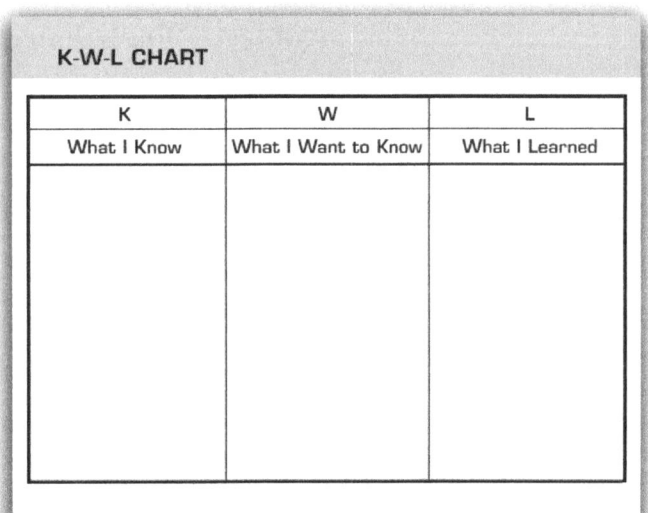

K-W-L Chart

Before you read a chapter, write down what you already know about a subject in the left column. Then write what you want to know in the center column. Then write what you learned in the last column. You can make a two-column version of this. Write what you know in the left and what you learned after reading the chapter.

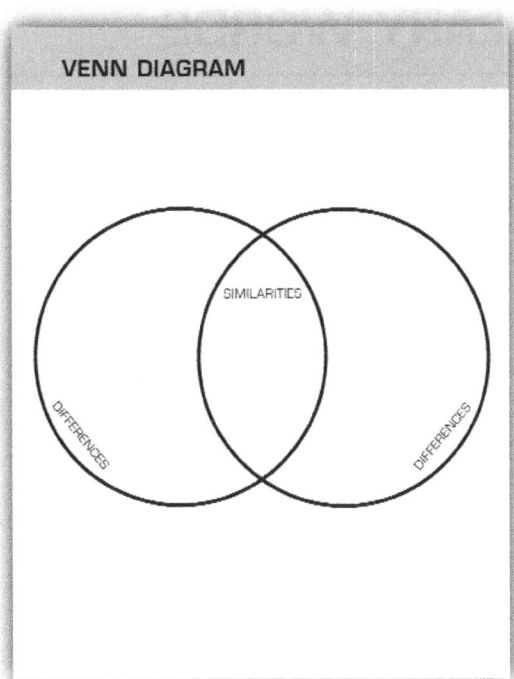

Venn Diagram

These overlapping circles show differences and similarities among topics. Each topic is shown as a circle. Any details the topics have in common go in the areas where those circles overlap. List the differences where the circles do not overlap.

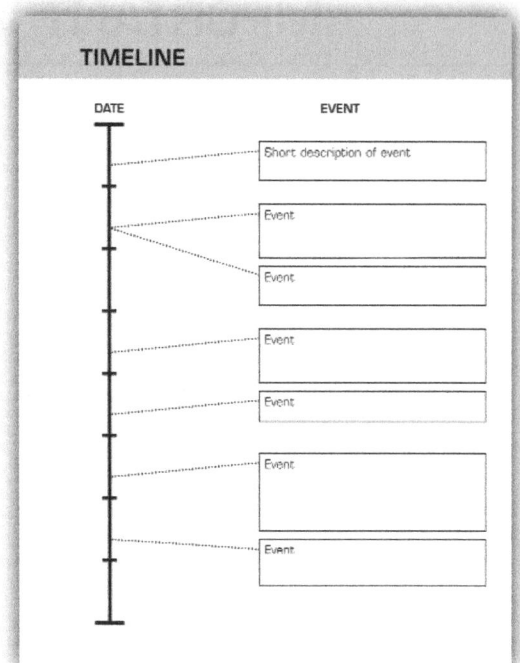

Timeline

A timeline divides a time period into equal chunks of time. Then it shows when events happened during that time. Decide how to divide up the timeline. Then write events in the boxes to the right when they happened. Connect them to the date line.

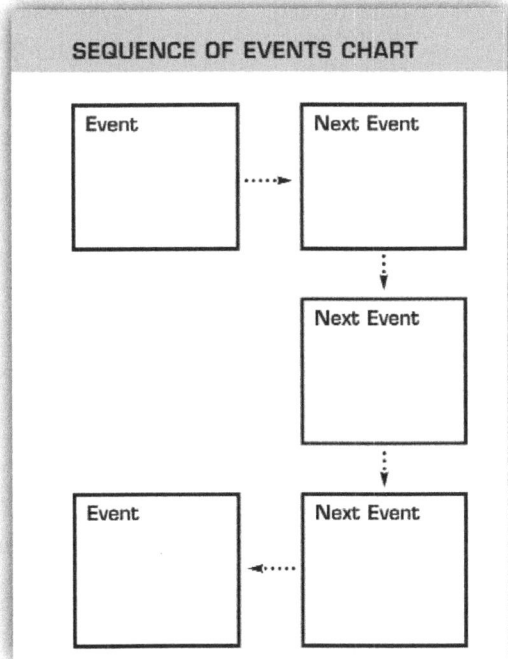

Sequence of Events Chart

Historical events bring about changes. These result in other events and changes. A sequence of events chart uses linked boxes to show how one event leads to another, and then another.

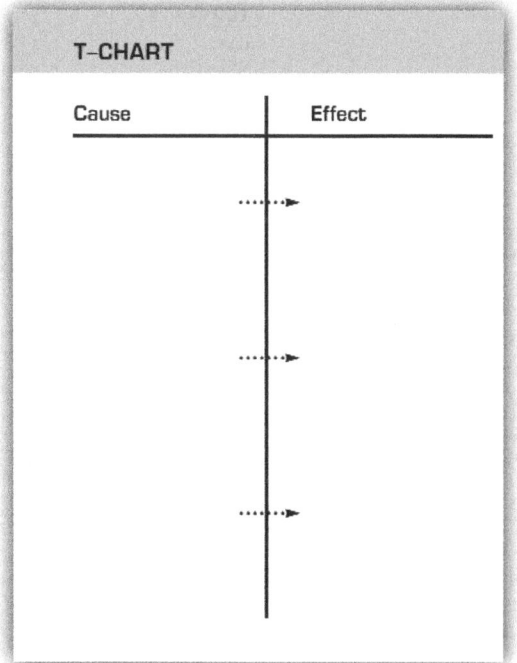

T–Chart

Use this chart to separate information into two columns. To separate causes and effects, list events, or causes, in one column. In the other column, list the change, or effect, each event brought about.

IMPORTANT VOCABULARY WORDS

The Word Bank section of each lesson will give you practice with important vocabulary words from the book. The words below are also important. They're listed in the order in which they appear in each chapter. Use a dictionary to look up any you don't know.

Chapter 1
wielding
barren
relentless
sacred
highlands
obsessively
nilometer
counterweight
caravan
expedition

Chapter 2
shriveled
palette
gateway
unification
symbolize
harmony

Chapter 3
unwieldy
manageable
dynasty
chaos
divine
parallel
mallet
anvil
papyrus
artisan
magnitude

Chapter 4
scribe
apprentice
privileged
breakthrough
fluent
cartouche

Chapter 5
shrine
stela
navigate
exquisitely
ma'at
sanctuary
ritual
mortuary

Chapter 6
afterlife
festering
meander
immortality
deceased
essential
fluids
embalmer

Chapter 7
disembark
swagger
plateau
restlessness
trafficked
lever
constellation
orientation
overseer
erosion
haunch

Chapter 8
luxurious
conceited
climate
bleak
rigid
centralized
botanist
eternity
draughtsman
monarchy
anarchy

Chapter 9
salve
millennia
barbaric
administer
accordance
absolved
malady
physician
prescription
tracheotomy
anesthesia
antibiotic
dosage
draught
asthmatic

Chapter 10
vertical
garrison
adapt
mercenaries
professional
besieged
gilded
siege

Chapter 11
colonnade
transform
divine
mortal
deity
trinket

frantic
vulnerable

Chapter 12
grooming
profile
conscious
accessory
supernatural
cosmetic
straightforward
destination
pedicure
alabaster
ceremony
meteoric
lyrics
ascertained

Chapter 13
essence
commemorate
scarab
commissioned
regal
vizier
deed
ambitious
turmoil
idyllic
elite
testimony
flogging
perjury

Chapter 14
rubble
antiquities
curator
hoax
seize
reputable
dispatches
priceless
correspondence
grievance
diplomacy
groveling
vassal
negotiations

Chapter 15
lion's share
ambassador
gratitude
archives
deformed
abscessed
revenues
differentiated

Chapter 16
restoration
replica
medley
sentinel
antechamber
torso
tuberculosis
vertebrae
fiber-optic
parasites

Chapter 17
boomerang
anxious
fastidious
pendant
pneumonia
descendants
frenzied

Chapter 18
insignificant
vile
infantrymen
vanquish
interrogated
rendezvous
isolated
infiltrated
plundering
reinforcements
stragglers
truce

Chapter 19
conveniences
accumulate
incense
frankincense
myrrh
willy-nilly
repel
niche
barter
company town
honeycomb
floodplain
toting
plummet
tunic

Chapter 20
deployed
ragamuffins
desperate
horde
slaughter
surrender
whirlwind

volley
maneuver
grappling hooks
capsize

Chapter 21
frontalism
innovator
mural
sacred ratio
galaxy
proportion
percussion
reveler
gyrating

Chapter 22
nomadic
earnest
contempt
legitimate
heir
coalition
valiant
battering ram
grievous
compassionate

Chapter 23
invincible
unmanageable
assassination
destined
flanked
uplifting
coronation
omen
oracle
dune

Chapter 24
magnitude
smugglers
forfeit
dowels
dabble
intermission
gusto
companionship
irresistible
adjacent
dissect
anatomy
autopsy
stellar

CHAPTER 1

YOU RULE: THE GEOGRAPHY OF EGYPT

CHAPTER SUMMARY

Life in ancient Egypt depended on the three-season cycle of the Nile River: *akhet, peret,* and *shemu.* Ancient Egyptians believed that their all-powerful pharaohs, or rulers, could speak to the gods and influence the cycle.

ACCESS

What is it like when one major geographic feature affects everything that you do? A chart will help you understand the cycles of the Nile. Read the chapter, and in your history journal create a three-column chart with the headings *Season, What the Nile Does,* and *What Egyptians Did and Felt.* List the three season cycles described on pages 15–17. Use information from the chapter to describe in the second and third columns how the Nile changed during each season and how the ancient Egyptians responded to the changes.

WITH A PARENT OR PARTNER

The ancient Egyptians depended so much on water from the Nile that they developed the nilometer to measure and compare yearly water levels. What are some of the instruments we use to measure things today? Ask a parent or older family member to help you think of four or five types of modern measuring devices. Write a sentence about each that describes what it measures and why we find it useful or important.

CAST OF CHARACTERS

Write an adjective to describe each character. Then explain why you chose that adjective.

Pharaoh Pepi (PEH-pee) II _____

_____

_____

Harkhuf (HAR-khoof) _____

_____

_____

WORD BANK

barren   rapids   gauge   anguish   sacrifices   caravans

Choose words from the Word Bank to complete the sentences. One word is not used at all.

To _____ is to measure something.

People traveled together in _____ through the desert.

A land that has no water becomes _____ .

Ancient worshipers made _____ to the gods.

The boat moved swiftly over the _____ .

WORD PLAY

Look up the word you did not use in a dictionary. In your history journal, write a sentence using that word.

ALL OVER THE MAP

Label the following geographic features on the map:

- Nile River
- desert
- Nile Delta
- Cataracts

Then answer the following questions:

1. How far up the Nile do you think the river was navigable by boat? _____

2. Draw arrows on the map to indicate which direction the river flows.

3. Trace in colored pencil any tributaries to the Nile.

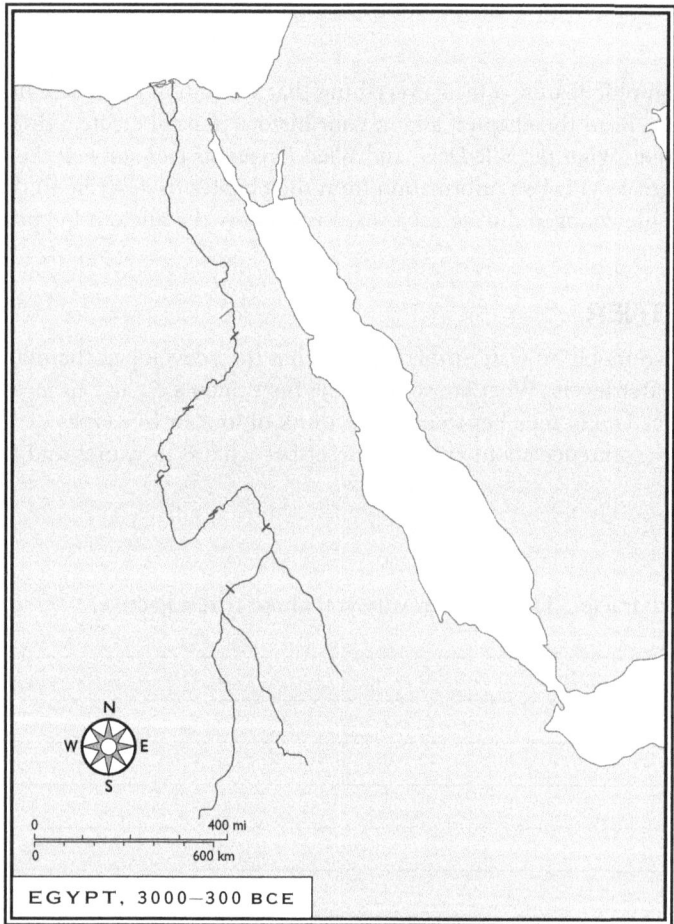

EGYPT, 3000–300 BCE

WORKING WITH PRIMARY SOURCES

Harkhuf's Tomb Inscription (about 2250 BCE)

We know a little about the interests and lifestyle of the boy king, Pepi II, from reading parts of his letters that are inscribed on Harkhuf's tomb. At the time of these writings, he was only eight years old and was supreme ruler of his world. He wrote to Harkhuf:

> Come north to the palace at once! Drop everything—hurry and bring that pygmy you have brought, alive, happy, and well, for the divine dances, to gladden the heart, to delight the heart of the king who lives for ever!

Imagine that you are supreme ruler of your world. In your history journal, write a paragraph describing a typical day in your royal life. Where do you spend the day? What do you eat? What kinds of things do you do?

CHAPTER 2

WRITTEN IN STONE: THE FIRST KING

CHAPTER SUMMARY

Ancient Egypt was once divided into two parts, Upper Egypt and Lower Egypt. The Narmer Palette (3100 BCE), an ancient stone carving, tells the story of the unification of Egypt under its first king.

ACCESS

Nekhen and Tjeni were villages that grew to be important towns in ancient Egypt. In your history journal, make two copies of the main idea map graphic organizer from page 8 of this study guide. In the center circle of one map, write *Nekhen*; in the other, write *Tjeni*. As you read the chapter, write details about these towns in the surrounding circles.

CAST OF CHARACTERS

Write a sentence or two about why the following character was important.

Narmer (NAR-mer) _____

_____

WORD BANK

palette   legend   conquered   chaos   pigments   harmony

Choose words from the Word Bank to complete the sentences. Two words are not used.

_____ describes a situation that is confused or disorganized.

A _____ is a popular story from history that may not be true.

The king and his army _____ the enemy forces.

People living in _____ are peaceful.

WORD PLAY

Look up the two words that you did not use in the dictionary. Write one sentence in the space below that includes both words.

_____

_____

WITH A PARENT OR PARTNER

The word *unification* begins with the prefix *uni-*, which means "one." In five minutes, write all the words you can think of that start with *uni-*. Ask a parent or partner to do the same. Then read your lists to each other. Look up in a dictionary any words either of you do not know.

ALL OVER THE MAP

Read the "Topsy Turvy" sidebar on page 23, and study the map. Then label the following geographical features and areas on this map.

Nile River   Mediterranean Sea   Red Sea   Upper Egypt   Lower Egypt

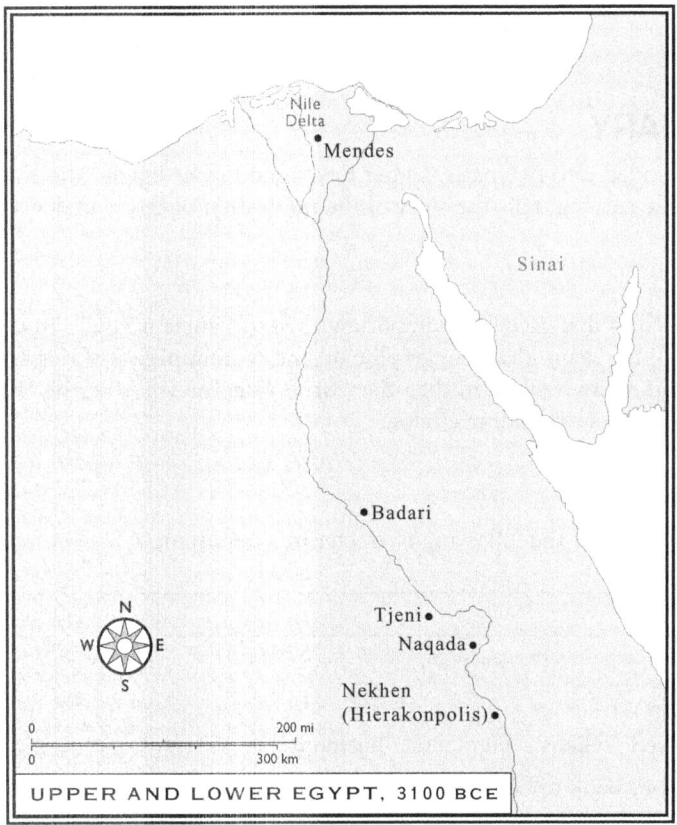

UPPER AND LOWER EGYPT, 3100 BCE

Answer the following questions in your history journal.

1. Why was ancient Egypt once called "The Two Lands"?

2. In which direction does the Nile River flow?

3. How does gravity affect the direction in which the Nile flows?

4. Why are the two parts of Egypt called "Upper" and "Lower"?

WORKING WITH PRIMARY SOURCES

The Narmer Palette (3100 BCE)

The creator of the Narmer Palette carved pictures and symbols into stone to tell the dramatic story of King Narmer's unification of the Two Lands. Read the description of the Narmer Palette on pages 24–26 and answer this question:

Why do the authors describe the Narmer Palette as being like a "comic book"?

_____

_____

_____

_____

On one or more pages in your history journal, using only pictures and symbols, create a "comic book" describing an important event in your life.

STAIRWAY TO HEAVEN: THE OLD KINGDOM

CHAPTER SUMMARY

The Old Kingdom Period (2686–2184 BCE) was a time of wealth and prosperity in ancient Egypt. During this period a brilliant architect, Imhotep, designed and built a burial complex for King Djoser that included the first pyramid.

ACCESS

Write the names of the characters below in a column in your history journal. As you read the chapter, write short sentences about why each person was important.

CAST OF CHARACTERS

Djoser (ZO-zer)

Manetho (MAN-eh-tho)

Imhotep (im-HOE-tep)

Edwin Smith

WHAT HAPPENED WHEN?

In a complete sentence, tell what happened on the following dates:

2700 BCE _____

1862 CE _____

GO FIGURE

How many years passed between these two events? _____

WORD BANK

granaries   architect   masons   inundation   artisan

Choose words from the Word Bank to complete the sentences. One word is not used at all. Go back to the book to check information.

1. _____ helped cut the stone for the pyramids.

2. During the time of the _____, the waters of the Nile rose.

3. An _____ designs buildings.

4. During years of good harvests, extra grain was stored in _____ .

Look up in a dictionary the word you did not use. Write a sentence using that word.

_____

_____

CRITICAL THINKING

FACT OR OPINION?

A fact is a statement that can be proved. An opinion judges things or people, but it cannot be proved or disproved. Make a two-column chart in your journal. Label one column *Fact* and the other column *Opinion*. Write each sentence below from the chapter in the column where it belongs.

1. Manetho grouped the kings into 30 ruling families that we call dynasties.

2. Even a god-king must feel awe at the sight of a structure larger than anything built before it . . .

3. The architect's name was Imhotep and he built the first pyramid.

4. The burial complex was as big as twenty-four soccer fields.

5. . . . once scholars start organizing there is no stopping them.

6. The king's granaries filled.

7. King Djoser must have traveled from the capital city of Memphis to the burial grounds at Saqqara now and again . . .

8. In the 19th century, a German scholar decided to group the dynasties.

WORKING WITH PRIMARY SOURCES

Edwin Smith Papyrus, 30th century BCE

Read the last two paragraphs of the chapter, including the excerpt from the Edwin Smith Papyrus. Then answer these questions in your history journal.

1. What were some of the reasons that building the pyramids was dangerous for the workers?

2. How do you think Imhotep discovered his medical treatments and cures?

WRITE ABOUT IT

Imagine you are a farmer who has come to Saqqara for the first time to help build the pyramid. What do you see when you arrive at the burial complex? What are the work conditions like? The weather? What foods do you eat? Write a paragraph in your history journal describing your experience.

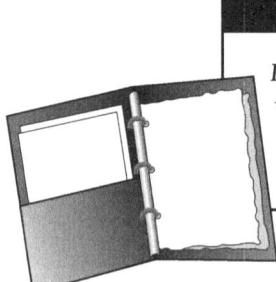

HISTORY JOURNAL

Don't forget to share your history journal with your classmates, and ask if you can see what their journals look like. You might be surprised—and get some new ideas.

THANK *YOU*, ROSETTA STONE: HIEROGLYPHS

CHAPTER SUMMARY

Ancient Egyptians may have been the first people to write, using pictures known as hieroglyphs to represent objects and sounds. But Egyptian forms of writing changed, and our ability to understand hieroglyphs was lost. The discovery of the Rosetta Stone (196 BCE) in 1799 enabled us to decipher the ancient words.

ACCESS

You may have seen pictures of Egyptian hieroglyphics before, in books or magazines, or even in movies. Perhaps their mysterious beauty made you curious to know more about them. In your history journal, copy the K-W-L graphic organizer chart from page 8 of this study guide. In the *What I Know* column, write what you already know about hieroglyphics. (If you don't know anything, that's okay.) In the *What I Want to Know* column, write three questions that you have. After reading the chapter, complete the *What I Learned* column with facts about hieroglyphics.

CAST OF CHARACTERS

Write a sentence or two about why each character was important.

Bekenkhons _____

_____

Ptolemy V (TALL-uh-mee) _____

_____

Napoleon _____

_____

Thomas Young _____

_____

WHAT HAPPENED WHEN?

In a complete sentence, tell what happened on the following dates:

About 3100 BCE _____

_____

196 BCE _____

_____

1799 CE _____

_____

DO THE MATH

Did the year 196 BCE come before or after 3100 BCE? _____

WORD BANK

demotics   hieroglyphics   hieratic

Choose words from the word bank to complete the sentences. One word is not used.

Egyptians first wrote in pictures called _____. A kind of shorthand, called

_____, eventually became popular for everyday writing.

WORD PLAY

The Egyptian cursive writing known as *sesh* was called *demotics* by the Greeks. The prefix *dem-*
comes from the Greek word *demotika*, which means "popular" or "of the people." Can you think of
another word we use that begins with *dem-* and relates to "the people"? Write the word here.

_____

WRITE ABOUT IT

What would it be like to create your own unique form of writing? What kinds of pictures or symbols
might you use? At the top of a page in your history journal, write a line from one of your favorite
songs. In the space below, write the line from the song again, this time using only pictures and
symbols that you create to express the meaning of the words.

COMPREHENSION
SEQUENCE OF EVENTS

These sentences describe the steps in making papyrus. Read the chapter and put
them in order by writing numbers in the blanks next to each event. (Write "1" next
to the earliest event, and so forth.)

_____ Cover the reed strips with linen, then pound the sheet with a mallet.

_____ Slice the stem into thin strips.

_____ The dried sap will glue the strips together.

_____ The crushed reeds ooze sticky sap.

_____ Lay the strips together, slightly overlapping.

_____ Peel the skin off the papyrus stem.

_____ Arrange another layer on top, going in the opposite direction.

_____ Glue the sheets together with flour and water paste.

When you have completed the exercise, make a sequence of events chart in your history journal
(see page 9 of this study guide). Draw it with eight boxes. Copy each event in a box, beginning
with the first one and ending with the last one.

WORKING WITH PRIMARY SOURCES

Inscription on a statue of Bekenkhons (1250 BCE)

Read the description on pages 36–37 of the life of a student scribe, ending with the details of the
inscription on the statue of Bekenkhons. Imagine that you are a teacher writing a report card for
young Bekenkhons, who is learning to be a scribe. Begin like this: "Bekenkhons works very hard to
learn his craft." Continue the report in your history journal. Be sure to list the kinds of things that
Bekenkhons has to learn to write about when he is a scribe, and grade him on them.

CHAPTER 5

IT'S A GOD-EAT-GOD WORLD: EGYPTIAN RELIGION

CHAPTER SUMMARY

Ancient Egyptians worshipped thousands of different gods. It was the job of the pharaoh and his priests to take care of the gods, and they built elaborate temples for this purpose.

ACCESS

Ancient Egyptians seemingly thought that everything had a god—things, objects in nature, subjects of learning, protection against dangers, and so on. If this ancient Egyptian belief were brought into the present, what would this new set of gods be like? What dangers would they protect against? What would be their purpose in different objects? List five such gods, what they effect, and what they might look like.

CAST OF CHARACTERS

Write a sentence or two about why each character was important.

Neferhotep (nef-er-HOE-tep) _____

_____

Plutarch (PLOO-tark) _____

_____

David O'Connor _____

William Petrie _____

_____

WHAT HAPPENED WHEN?

In a complete sentence, tell what happened on the following dates:

1741–1730 BCE _____

1st century CE _____

1967 CE _____

WORD BANK

shrines   sacred   archaeologist   stela   scarab   excavate

Choose words from the Word Bank to complete these sentences. Two words are not used.

A _____ is a type of beetle (insect).

A slab of rock inscribed with an ancient story is called a _____.

Statues of gods were kept in _____.

An _____ searches for and studies ancient artifacts to learn about human life in the past.

WORD PLAY

Look up in a dictionary the words you did not use. Write a sentence in your history journal using each word.

COMPREHENSION

In the first five chapters you have read about the ancient Egyptian concept of *ma'at*, or "balance." Balance in life was extremely important. Look back through the first few chapters and reread the descriptions of *ma'at*. Then, in your history journal, answer the following questions in complete sentences.

1. Why was balance so important to the ancient Egyptians?

2. Is balance important in your life? If so, what kinds of balance are important to you, and why?

WRITE ABOUT IT

Because they protected and served the gods, temple priests were very important in ancient Egypt. Read the descriptions of the lives of temple priests and their duties in this chapter, then imagine that you could interview a temple priest. Using a two-column chart, write your questions and the answers that you think a temple priest might give. Be sure to give your priest a name.

WORKING WITH PRIMARY SOURCES

Read the interview of archaeologist David O'Connor on pages 48–49, and answer the following questions, using complete sentences.

1. Why is Egypt a good place to learn about early cultures?

   _____

   _____

2. Why are winter and spring good times of year to excavate in Egypt?

   _____

   _____

3. What are some of the dangers archaeologists face when excavating a site?

   _____

   _____

4. Why is it important to record exactly where artifacts are found?

   _____

   _____

5. What kind of scientist can tell where a certain type of wood came from?

   _____

   _____

GROUP TOGETHER

Wouldn't it be fun to know what other students think about Ancient Egyptian religious beliefs? Get a few friends together and ask your teacher to help you organize a discussion group at school. Have one person take notes and another person present the group's ideas to the class.

6

IT'S A WRAP: MUMMIES AND THE AFTERLIFE

CHAPTER SUMMARY

Egyptians believed that their only chance for a happy afterlife was to gain entrance to the Field of Reeds. Everyone had three spirits that each played a different role in achieving this. Because the spirits needed their bodies intact, Egyptians developed mummification.

ACCESS

Egyptians believed that everyone had three spirits: the *Ba*, the *Ka*, and the *Akh*. Each spirit had very unique qualities or tasks that helped achieve a good afterlife. Copy the outline graphic organizer from page 8 of this study guide. On each main idea line, write the name of a spirit. List facts about each spirit on the detail lines as you read the chapter.

CAST OF CHARACTERS

Write in complete sentences why each character was important.

Herodotus (huh-RAH-duh-tus) _____

_____

Diodorus (die-uh-DOR-us) Siculus (SICK-u-lus) _____

_____

COMPREHENSION

Look for Herodotus and Diodorus Siculus in the Cast of Characters on pages 9–11. Read their brief descriptions and answer the following questions in complete sentences in your history journal.

1. What part of the world were Herodotus and Diodorus Siculus from?
2. How did Diodorus Siculus contribute to our knowledge of world history?
3. What is Herodotus known as?

WHAT HAPPENED WHEN?

In a complete sentence, tell what happened on the following dates:

about 2375–2184 BCE _____

about 1500–250 BCE _____

WORD BANK

mummification

Look up the definitions of *mummy*, *mummify*, and *mummification* in a dictionary. Write each word in a sentence in your history journal.

CRITICAL THINKING
CAUSE AND EFFECT

Egyptians believed that after they died they had to pass a series of tests to enter the Field of Reeds. After you read the chapter, copy the T-chart graphic organizer from page 9 of this workbook into your history journal. Copy the causes below into the first column. Then find the effect of each cause in the chapter and write the effect in the second column.

1. The spirits correctly answered the questions of the gatekeepers.

2. The spirits successfully declared their innocence before 42 gods.

3. The dead person's heart balanced with truthfulness and justice.

4. The dead person's heart weighed heavy with sin.

WITH A PARENT OR PARTNER

After completing your chart, read the matched pairs aloud to a parent or partner, connected by the word *so*.

WORKING WITH PRIMARY SOURCES

Pyramid Texts (about 2375–2184 BCE)

Coffin Texts (Middle Kingdom)

Book of the Dead (about 1500–250 BCE)

The Pyramid Texts, the Coffin Texts, and the Book of the Dead are documents from three different periods of Egyptian history that tell us about Egyptian burial practices and beliefs about the afterlife. Create a three-circle Venn diagram in your history journal using the model on page 9 of this study guide. In the middle of each circle, write the name of one of these periods of history: *Old Kingdom*, *Middle Kingdom*, *New Kingdom*. Then write each of the details below in the correct circles. If details apply to more than one period, write them in the overlapping parts of the circles.

- spells written on sides of coffins
- Book of the Dead
- only pharaohs allowed into Field of Reeds
- Coffin Texts
- Field of Reeds open to all
- spells written on scrolls
- kings had to answer questions
- Pyramid Texts
- scrolls buried with the body
- kings had answers and spells buried with them

WRITE ABOUT IT

Read the description of the mummification process on pages 54–56. Then answer the following questions in complete sentences.

1. What bodily organ did the Egyptians believe was most important?

_____

_____

2. How long might it take to wrap a body in linen?

_____

_____

3. Why was it important for the mummy to have a painted mask that looked like the dead person's face?

_____

_____

4. What kind of salt was used to dry out the body?

_____

_____

TOMB BUILDERS: THE PYRAMID AGE/THE OLD KINGDOM

CHAPTER SUMMARY

The Great Pyramid was built more than 4,000 years ago as a tomb and a stairway to the afterlife for the king Khufu. It took thousands of workers more than 20 years to complete. The Great Sphinx, a massive statue with the body of a lion and the head of a man, guards the pyramids at Giza.

ACCESS

How do you think the Great Pyramid could have been built with no modern machinery? What was the purpose of the pyramids, or the Sphinx? In your history journal, copy the K-W-L graphic organizer from page 8 of this study guide. In the *What I Know* column, write anything you may already know about the Great Pyramid, the Sphinx, or the other pyramids at Giza. In the *What I Want to Know* column, write three questions that you have. After reading the chapter, complete the *What I Learned* column with facts about the Giza pyramid complex.

CAST OF CHARACTERS

Read the chapter and write a complete sentence about why each character was important.

Khufu (COO-foo) _____

_____

Thutmose (TUT-moze) IV _____

_____

WHAT HAPPENED WHEN?

In a complete sentence, tell what happened during this time period.

about 1419–1386 BCE _____

_____

WORD BANK

Mennefer   mer   mummy

Complete the sentences below with words from the Word Bank. One word is not used.

1. _____, the capital city of ancient Egypt, was near modern-day Cairo.

2. King Khufu's _____ was part of an elaborate burial complex.

WORD PLAY

Write a sentence that includes the word not used. (If necessary, look this word up in a dictionary).

_____

_____

DO THE MATH

1. How many pounds equal 1 ton? _____

2. How many pounds would a 40-ton stone block weigh? _____

COMPREHENSION

SEQUENCE OF EVENTS

How did the builders of the Great Pyramid move those massive stones into place? In your history journal, copy the sequence of events chart on page 9 of this study guide. The final event is placing a block of stone in place on the pyramid. Working backward, fill in the other boxes with the steps that led to this final event.

WORKING WITH PRIMARY SOURCES

Read the story of the Sphinx and the Dream Stela on page 63. Then answer these questions in complete sentences.

1. What protected the Sphinx from crumbling for thousands of years?

_____

_____

2. What does the Dream Stela describe?

_____

_____

3. What deal does the Sphinx make with Prince Thutmose?

_____

_____

4. Why might Thutmose have made up the story of his dream?

_____

_____

We know from a small patch of color near one of the Sphinx's ears that it used to be brightly painted. What do you think it looked like? In your history journal, draw a picture of the Sphinx. Use markers or colored pencils to color the Sphinx the way you think it might have originally been painted, or how you'd like to see it painted now.

WITH A PARENT OR PARTNER

The Great Pyramid at Giza is one of the Seven Wonders of the Ancient World, and the only one still standing. Ask a parent or partner to help you do an Internet search for information on the Seven Wonders of the Ancient World. In your history journal list the Seven Wonders, and write in a complete sentence at least one fact about each. Then, with your partner, try to think of seven modern wonders that might be the equal of the ancient wonders.

HISTORY JOURNAL

Don't forget to share your history journal with your classmates, and ask if you can see what their journals look like. You might be surprised—and get some new ideas.

CHAPTER 8

FROM MONARCHY TO ANARCHY AND BACK AGAIN: THE FIRST INTERMEDIATE PERIOD AND THE MIDDLE KINGDOM

CHAPTER SUMMARY

The First Intermediate Period was a time of political turmoil as well as greater intellectual freedom and new religious and cultural ideas and technologies. Royal power, peace, and prosperity returned to Egypt during the Middle Kingdom.

ACCESS

During the First Intermediate Period, power shifted from the king to the governors of the Egyptian provinces. Imagine that you could interview an Egyptian governor during this time. Before reading, skim through the chapter. Then in your history journal make a list of five questions you would ask the governor (be sure to give him a name!). One question might be, "How did you become so wealthy?" Now read the chapter carefully and write the answers to the questions as you imagine your governor might answer them.

CAST OF CHARACTERS

Write a complete sentence about why each character is important.

Pepi (PEH-pee) II _____

Ankhtyfy (ANKH-tee-fee) _____

Sinuhe (SIN-oo-way) _____

Amenemhet (ah-MEN-em-het) I _____

Senwosert (SEN-whe-sert) I _____

WHAT HAPPENED WHEN?

In a complete sentence, tell what happened on these dates:

2278 BCE _____

about 1991–1926 BCE _____

TIMELINE

Make a timeline using the timeline graphic organizer on page 9 of this study guide. Starting at the top, divide the timeline into three periods: the Old Kingdom, the First Intermediate Period, and the Middle Kingdom. Then place the following characters or events from the chapter on the timeline, drawing lines connecting them to the appropriate periods.

return of centralized power	Ankhtyfy governed
vertical loom invented	two provinces
Pepi II's reign	end of Pepi II's reign

WORD BANK

monarchy   anarchy   intermediate   drought

Choose words from the word bank to complete the sentences. One word is not used at all.

1. _____ is the absence of governmental authority.

2. A country that is ruled by a king is a _____.

3. Something that happens in between two events is _____.

WITH A PARENT OR PARTNER

The prefix *inter* means "between." In five minutes, write all the words you can think of that start with *inter*. Ask a parent or partner to do the same. Then read your lists to each other. Look up in a dictionary any words either of you do not know.

CRITICAL THINKING
COMPARE AND CONTRAST

Life during the First Intermediate Period is generally considered to have been difficult and chaotic, but it had its good points, too. Read the chapter and sort these varying descriptions into the organizer below.

- people began to think for themselves
- "festering from civil wars"
- others besides the king might enter the afterlife
- artists painted in new styles
- artisans no longer told how things must be done
- "bathed in blood"
- "mercy has perished"
- inventions such as the vertical loom

FIRST INTERMEDIATE PERIOD

POSITIVE	NEGATIVE

WORKING WITH PRIMARY SOURCES

Although the Middle Kingdom was politically more stable than the First Intermediate Period, *The Tale of Sinuhe* tells us that there were still constant threats to the monarchy. Read the story of Sinuhe on page 68.

MAKING INFERENCES

Why did Sinuhe flee Egypt when he heard that King Amenemhet had been murdered? Give your answer in complete sentences.

_____

_____

Copy the outline graphic organizer on page 8 of this study guide in your history journal to create an outline of the life of Sinuhe. Write the main idea of *The Tale of Sinuhe* in a complete sentence at the top of your outline. Write two details in complete sentences, labeled Detail A and Detail B, under each of these topics:

Topic I: Sinuhe leaves Egypt

Topic II: Sinuhe's life outside of Egypt

Topic III: Sinuhe's return to Egypt

TAKE TWO MICE AND CALL ME IN THE MORNING: MEDICINE AND MAGIC

CHAPTER SUMMARY

Ancient Egyptian medicine combined science and magic to treat illnesses and had some surprising similarities to modern Western medicine.

ACCESS

Can you imagine what it would be like to be treated for illness by a doctor in ancient Egypt? What kinds of treatments might she use? Use the K-W-L graphic organizer on page 8 of this study guide to begin to explore ancient Egyptian medicine. In the *What I Know* column, write everything you already know on the subject (if you don't know anything, that's okay). Fill in the *What I Want to Know* column with questions, and as you read the chapter, write the answers to your questions and other interesting facts in the *What I Learned* column.

CAST OF CHARACTERS

Write a complete sentence about why each character is important.

Homer _____

_____

Diodorus (die-uh-DOR-us) Siculus (SICK-u-lus) _____

_____

Herodotus (huh-RAH-duh-tus) _____

_____

WHAT HAPPENED WHEN?

In a complete sentence, tell what happened on the dates below:

about 1600 BCE _____

about 1550 BCE _____

about 750 BCE _____

WORD BANK

peru-ankh   Sekhmet   obsidian

Choose a word from the Word Bank to complete the sentences below. One word is not used at all.

1. A _____ was a medical school, or "house of life," where Egyptian doctors studied medical records and texts.

2. Egyptian doctors used surgical instruments made from _____, a volcanic glass.

WORD PLAY

There were unhappy consequences for an Egyptian doctor who did not follow the medical rules in prescribing treatments. Today if a doctor mistreats a patient we call it *malpractice*. The prefix *mal-* means "bad." Look in a dictionary for three more words that begin with *mal-* and refer to something bad. (You'll be able to tell by their definitions.) Write the words and their definitions in your history journal, then write a complete sentence for each word.

CRITICAL THINKING
COMPARE AND CONTRAST

Comparisons of ancient Egyptian medicine and modern Western medicine show both stark contrasts and surprising similarities. A graphic organizer can help you understand what the two have in common. Create a two-circle Venn diagram like the one on page 9 of this study guide. Label one circle *Egyptian Medicine* and the other circle *Modern Medicine*. Read the chapter and then copy the words or phrases below in the correct circles. Any descriptions that apply to both types of medicine belong in the overlapping area.

vaccines	medical textbooks studied	surgery performed
evil spirits cause illness	doctors specialize	broken bones set
excrement used as medicine	herbal medicines used	amputations performed
doctors study many years	man-made antibiotics used	anesthesia given
obsidian instruments used	pulse checked	medication dosages adjusted

WRITE ABOUT IT

The Egyptians had interesting treatments for a variety of medical problems that we are familiar with today. In your history journal, create a chart with two columns. Label the first column *Health Problem* and the second column *Treatment*. Write the health problems listed below in the first column, and then read the chapter to find out how the Egyptians would have treated them. Write each treatment in the second column.

asthma cough cold indigestion cut heart attack

LETTER TO A FRIEND

Think of a health problem for which a doctor has treated you or someone you know. How do you think an Egyptian doctor might have tried to cure the problem? Imagine that you are an ancient Egyptian who wants to recommend a doctor and his treatment to a friend. In your history journal, write a letter to your friend that describes your illness and what medicines or magic the doctor used to make you well.

GROUP TOGETHER

Wouldn't it be fun to know what other students think about medicine in ancient Egypt? Get a few friends together and ask your teacher to help you organize a discussion group at school. Have one person take notes and another person present the group's ideas to the class.

HANDS OFF:
THE SECOND INTERMEDIATE PERIOD

CHAPTER SUMMARY

The Second Intermediate Period was a time of conflict between the Egyptians and the Hyksos, an immigrant people who were skilled warriors and who built the walled fortress city of Avaris in the Nile Delta.

ACCESS

The Hyksos were different from the Egyptians in many ways. Read the descriptions of the Hyksos in the opening pages of the chapter. To help you understand them, use the main idea map graphic organizer on page 8 of this study guide. In the large circle, write *The Hyksos*. In several connecting smaller circles, write individual details about the Hyksos and the changes they brought to Egypt.

CAST OF CHARACTERS

Write a complete sentence about why each character is important.

Manetho (MAN-eh-tho) _____

Seqenenre (seck-EN-en-re) _____

Ahmose (AHK-moz) _____

Ahhotep (ah-HOE-tep) I _____

Josephus (jo-SEE-fus) _____

WHAT HAPPENED WHEN?

In a complete sentence, tell what happened on the dates below.

about 1574–1550 BCE _____

about 1550 BCE _____

about 1212–1202 BCE _____

about 300 BCE _____

TIMELINE

By the end of Chapter 10 you will have learned about the first five ancient Egyptian time periods. Using the timeline graphic organizer on page 9 of this study guide, create a timeline in your history journal that includes the time periods below, in correct order. (Start at the top of the timeline and work your way down.) Include the approximate dates for each period, which can be found in the Top Ten Periods sidebar on page 28 in Chapter 3.

First Intermediate Period   **Old Kingdom Period**   **Early Dynastic Period**

Middle Kingdom Period   **Second Intermediate Period**

WORD BANK

heqa-khasut   scribe   chiefs of foreign lands

Choose words from the Word Bank to complete the sentences. One word is not used at all.

Hyksos is the Greek word for _____, which was the Egyptian name of the foreigners who built the city of Avaris. In Egyptian, the name means _____.

COMPREHENSION

Read the sidebar Women in Battle on page 80, and in your history journal answer these questions in complete sentences.

1. How long did Queen Ahhotep I live?
2. Do you think it was typical for someone to live that long in ancient Egypt?

WITH A PARENT OR PARTNER

With an older family member, do an Internet search using the phrase "ancient Egypt average lifespan." Read three sources that you find and write a paragraph answering the following question in your history journal. After you answer the question, briefly list your sources and their Web addresses.

How long did the average ancient Egyptian live?

CRITICAL THINKING
CAUSE AND EFFECT

Below is a list of causes and effects from the chapter having to do with war between the Egyptians and the Hyksos. Copy the T-chart graphic organizer from page 9 of this study guide into your history journal. Insert the facts below in proper order in the organizer.

CAUSES	EFFECTS
• The Egyptians trained to improve their skills. • Egyptians did not want to fight and die away from home. • King Seqenenre was insulted by the Hyksos king's complaints about the royal hippos. • The Egyptians were farmers and the Hyksos were professional soldiers with body armor, leather helmets, and powerful bows.	• Egypt went to war with the Hyksos. • The Hyksos won the first battles with the Egyptians. • The Egyptians became an organized military power. • The king hired foreign mercenaries to fight battles outside of Egypt.

ALL OVER THE MAP
LOCATION

Using what you have learned so far about ancient Egypt, label the geographic features and locations listed below on the map.

Red Sea

Upper Egypt

Lower Egypt

Avaris

Nile River

Mediterranean Sea

Delta

Thebes

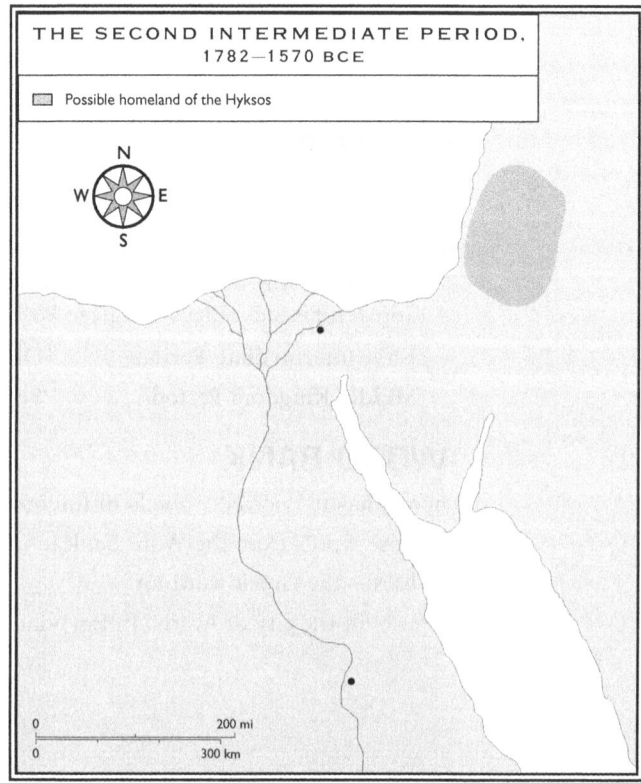

THE SECOND INTERMEDIATE PERIOD,
1782–1570 BCE

▦ Possible homeland of the Hyksos

0   200 mi
0   300 km

CHAPTER 11

A TALE OF TWO DEITIES: HATSHEPSUT AND THUTMOSE III

CHAPTER SUMMARY

To be accepted as ruler, Queen Hatshepsut had to transform herself into a king by creating myths about her divinity and dressing in masculine clothing. She was followed by Thutmose III, whose military skills reinforced Egyptians' belief that he was divine.

ACCESS

Was it fair that Queen Hatshepsut had to dress like a man and make up stories about herself to be accepted as ruler? Do you think that conditions are better today for women in positions of political power, or in some ways the same? In your history journal, write a paragraph expressing your thoughts about how things may or may not have changed for women since Hatshepsut's time. After you have written your paragraph, create a main idea map graphic organizer like the one on page 8 of this study guide. In the central circle, write *Queen Hatshepsut*. Read the chapter, and in the connecting circles write some of the things Hatshepsut had to do to become king.

WITH A PARENT OR PARTNER

You may wish to talk about the subject of women and power with a parent or a friend. Share and compare your ideas.

CAST OF CHARACTERS

Write a complete sentence about why each character is important.

Hatshepsut (hat-SHEP-soot)_____

_____

Thutmose (TUT-moze) II _____

_____

Thutmose (TUT-moze) III _____

_____

WHAT HAPPENED WHEN?

In a complete sentence, tell what happened on the dates below.

1504 BCE _____

1483 BCE _____

WORD BANK

Choose words from the Word Bank to complete the sentences. One word is not used at all.

mortal   divine   destiny

Ancient Egyptians believed that their rulers were _____, or godlike, and that

ordinary people were _____, or mere human beings with no special powers.

WORD PLAY

Look up in a dictionary the word that you did not use. Write that word in a sentence.

COMPREHENSION
SEQUENCE OF EVENTS

Read the story of the trade expedition to Punt on pages 83–85. Imagine the surprise the Egyptian traders must have felt when they saw the jungle landscape that was so different from their desert home. In your history journal, make a sequence of events graphic organizer like the one on page 9 of this study guide, and then write these sentences about the expedition in the correct order.

Villagers show Egyptian traders where to find ebony and incense.

Traders meet village chief.

Small boats are loaded with items to trade.

Egyptian traders come to a village in Punt.

Sailors unload riches from Punt.

Traders give villagers gifts.

Five sailing ships leave Egypt.

List at least five other items besides ebony and incense that the Egyptians brought back from Punt.

MAKING INFERENCES

The chapter explains that Hatshepsut accepted all the riches brought back from Punt "as her due, in the name of Egypt and her godly father Amun." What do you think the phrase *as her due* means? Why would Hatshepsut feel this way? Write a complete sentence about it in your history journal.

WORKING WITH PRIMARY SOURCES

Tomb Inscription of an Army Scribe, Deir el-Bahri (about 1479 BCE)

Of King Thutmose III a scribe wrote, "I recorded the victories the king won in every land, putting them in writing according to the facts."

To the Egyptians, Thutmose III was a military hero whose skill and daring proved his divinity. After you read the chapter, use the outline graphic organizer on page 8 of this study guide to tell the story of his victory at the city of Megiddo. Start by writing the main idea of the story in a complete sentence at the top of the page. Then write two or more important details in complete sentences beneath each of these topics:

• Topic I: Why it was important to regain control of Megiddo

• Topic II: The decision about which road to take

• Topic III: What happened when the Egyptians reached Megiddo

READ MORE

To learn more about Hatshepsut and Thutmose III, see the Further Reading suggestions at the end of *The Ancient Egyptian World.*

IN STYLE ALONG THE NILE: DAILY LIFE

CHAPTER SUMMARY

Daily life in ancient Egypt had some similarities to our daily American life, but there were many differences.

ACCESS

What do you already know about daily life in ancient Egypt? How did people dress? What were some of the challenges? Use the K-W-L graphic organizer on page 8 of this study guide to begin to think about daily life in ancient Egypt. In the *What I Know* column, write everything you already know on the subject. Fill in the *What I Want to Know* column with questions, and as you read the chapter, write the answers to your questions and other interesting facts about daily life in ancient Egypt in the *What I Learned* column.

CAST OF CHARACTERS

Write a complete sentence about why this character is important.

Herodotus (huh-RAH-duh-tus)_____

MAKING INFERENCES

Which of the following pharaohs wore a fake beard? (Circle one.)

Pepi II

Thutmose III

Hatshepsut

Why did this pharaoh wear a fake beard?

_____

_____

WHAT HAPPENED WHEN?

In a complete sentence, tell what happened on each date below.

about 2345–2181 BCE_____

_____

about 2000 BCE_____

_____

about 1550 BCE _____

_____

WORD BANK

linen   barbarian   alabaster   rituals   fragrances   flax

Complete the paragraph below by writing the words from above in the blanks. One of the words is not used.

An uncivilized person, or _____, would probably not wear fine

_____ woven from _____ or use body oils made with

pleasant-smelling _____ like cinnamon or vanilla. He would certainly not own a

beautiful makeup jar carved from the delicate stone known as _____.

WORD PLAY

Look up in a dictionary the word that you did not use. Write a sentence using the word.

_____

CRITICAL THINKING

Imagine that you are an Egyptian preparing to go to a party at the pharaoh's palace. You want to be sure to do all the right things to look fashionable. Each of the beauty rituals listed is either an ancient Egyptian fashion "do" or a fashion "don't." Read the chapter and then write *Do* or *Don't* on the line beside each ritual.

_____ Wear gold or silver jewelry.

_____ Wear your hair long.

_____ Wear your sandals outdoors.

_____ Wear a palm frond wig.

_____ Tie a scented wax cone on top of your head.

_____ Wear eye makeup.

_____ Put chopped lettuce on your bald spot.

_____ Wear leather.

_____ Shave your beard.

WORKING WITH PRIMARY SOURCES
WRITE ABOUT IT

Last will and testament of Lady Naunakhte (about 1151–1145 BCE)

Lady Naunakhte was a "free woman of Egypt." How do you think the rights of ancient Egyptian women compare with women's rights in America today? After you read the chapter, write a paragraph in your history journal that describes Egyptian women's rights in the following areas: personal property, marriage, divorce.

Ancient Egyptians loved to wear jewelry. Look at the pictures of art and hieroglyphics throughout *The Ancient Egyptian World* for design ideas, and in your history journal describe or draw a design for a necklace that an ancient Egyptian might wear.

NAME THAT TOMB: AMENHOTEP III AND THE GOVERNMENT OF EGYPT

CHAPTER SUMMARY

The reign of Amenhotep III was a time of great prosperity for Egypt. Most of the wealth was controlled and enjoyed by the small upper classes, and the bulk of the population was unskilled and poor. Crimes were brutally punished.

ACCESS

There was a very clear social order in ancient Egypt that ranged from the king at the very top all the way to the many poor, illiterate people at the bottom. In your history journal draw a Social Order Pyramid with five layers. Write the name of the king, Amenhotep III, in the smallest layer at the very top, and place the poor people in the largest bottom layer. Fill in the middle three layers of the social order pyramid, from highest to lowest, with the people or groups described on page 98.

CAST OF CHARACTERS

Write an adjective that describes each character. Then write a complete sentence about why you chose that adjective.

	Adjective	Why?

Amenhotep (ah-men-HOE-tep) III _____

_____

Tiy (tee) _____

_____

WHAT HAPPENED WHEN?

The chapter describes four scarabs that were inscribed with details of historic events from Amenhotep III's reign. For each scarab listed below, write the Egyptian calendar year of Amenhotep's reign when it was created. (Remember, the Egyptians reset the calendar to year one every time a new king took the throne.) Then briefly describe the event that the scarab commemorated.

	Year	Event Commemorated

Scarab 1 _____

_____

Scarab 2 _____

_____

Scarab 3 _____

_____

Scarab 4 _____

_____

GO FIGURE

Approximately how old would Amenhotep III have been in Year 5 of his reign?

_____

WORD BANK

amputation   elite   vizier   illiterate   harem

Complete the sentences below using words from the Word Bank above in the blanks. One of the words is not used.

A _____ was a group of women who were part of the king's household.

The _____ kept the government running smoothly for the king.

People who cannot read or write are _____.

_____ is the cutting off of a body part.

WORD PLAY

Look up in a dictionary the word you did not use. Write a complete sentence using the word.

CRITICAL THINKING

We know from ancient documents that crimes were brutally punished in ancient Egypt. The chart lists some of the crimes people committed. Read the chapter. In the second column write the punishments that would have been suffered for committing these acts.

CRIME	PUNISHMENT
Tax evasion	
Stealing cattle	
Perjury	

List three other forms of punishment for crimes committed in ancient Egypt.

1. _____
2. _____
3. _____

WORKING WITH PRIMARY SOURCES

Histories, by Diodorus Siculus (about 90–21 BCE)

Diodorus Siculus wrote,

> The penalty for perjury was death; the reasoning being that the perjurer was guilty of the two greatest sins, being impious toward the gods and breaking the most important pledge known to man.

What is *perjury*? Look the word up in a dictionary and write a sentence that shows the meaning of the word.

MAKING INFERENCES

Diodorus Siculus says in this passage that a perjurer was guilty of two great sins. The first sin was impiety, which meant being irreverent or disrespectful to the gods. The second sin was "breaking the most important pledge known to man." What might "the most important pledge known to man" be? Why might ancient Egyptians believe that people who broke this pledge deserved death as punishment? Answer these questions in a paragraph in your history journal, and explain your thoughts.

COMPREHENSION
WITH A PARENT OR PARTNER

The king's vizier was a man or woman of extraordinary influence and power. Use the main idea map graphic organizer on page 8 of this study guide and work with a parent or partner to explore the power of the vizier. Write *vizier* in the central circle. Then fill in the surrounding circles with words or phrases from the chapter that describe some of the vizier's many titles and responsibilities.

DIPLOMACY MAKES GOOD FERTILIZER: FOREIGN RELATIONS DURING THE NEW KINGDOM

CHAPTER SUMMARY

The clay tablets known as the Amarna Letters have been identified as ancient diplomatic messages. This correspondence tells us a great deal about the political alliances and arguments between the New Kingdom pharaohs and rulers of other lands.

ACCESS

What would be so important to a government that it would record it on long-lasting media and keep it locked up in a special building? What would we learn about the government if those records were opened up thousands of years later? Read the description of the Amarna Letters that begins on page 101. In your history journal, make a list of at least 10 facts about the letters and their contents.

CAST OF CHARACTERS

After reading the chapter, write a complete sentence about how each character was involved in the story of the Amarna Letters.

E. A. Wallis Budge _____

Monsieur Grebaut _____

Nimmuriya (Amenhotep III) _____

Tiy _____

WHAT HAPPENED WHEN?

In a complete sentence, tell what happened on the following dates:

1386–1334 BCE _____

1887 CE _____

1894–1924 CE _____

WORD BANK

curator   dominion   antiquities   diplomacy   alliance   steamer

Complete the sentences below by writing the words from the Word Bank above in the blanks. Two of the words are not used.

_____ is the practice of negotiation between nations.

All the lands that the king ruled were part of his _____.

Nations that have an _____ agree to work together.

The _____ of a museum oversees the care of its collections of artifacts.

WORD PLAY

Look up in a dictionary the words you did not use. In your history journal, write complete sentences using the words.

COMPREHENSION
SEQUENCE OF EVENTS

The story of E. A. Wallis Budge's search for the Amarna Letters is like an adventure novel with a comic twist. Use the sequence of events graphic organizer on page 9 of this study guide to put the events from the chapter listed below in the proper order from beginning to end.

- Monsieur Grebaut had Budge followed in Egypt.
- Budge managed to take some of the Amarna Letters back to England.
- The British Museum sent Budge to Egypt to find the tablets discovered in Amarna.
- The steamer captain and the villagers delayed Monsieur Grebaut's delivery of an arrest warrant to Budge.
- Budge discovered that the Amarna tablets were diplomatic letters.

WORKING WITH PRIMARY SOURCES

Amarna Letters (about 1386–1334 BCE)

In a letter to Amenhotep III, the king of Babylon wrote,

> When I wrote to you about marrying your daughter you wrote to me saying, "From time immemorial no daughter of the king of Egypt has been given in marriage to anyone." Why do you say this? You are the king and you may do as you please. If you were to give a daughter, who would say anything about it?"

In some parts of the world, marriage is still used to strengthen alliances between groups of people or rulers. Do you think this practice is a good or a bad idea? How do you think the two people being married would feel about it? Write a paragraph in your history journal that expresses your thoughts on this subject.

ALL OVER THE MAP
INTERACTION

1. Label the following cities, countries, and geographic features on the map below.

Persian Gulf	Lakhish	Amarna	Red Sea
Babylon (city)	Euphrates River	Black Sea	Opel (Luxor)
Greece	Crete	Mycenae	Cyprus
Ugarit	Knossos	Tigris River	Aegean Sea
Nile River	Mediterranean Sea	Hattuss	Troy

2. Use patterns or shading to indicate the following nations. Then key your patterns to the legend.

MITTANI   EGYPT   BABYLONIA   HATTI

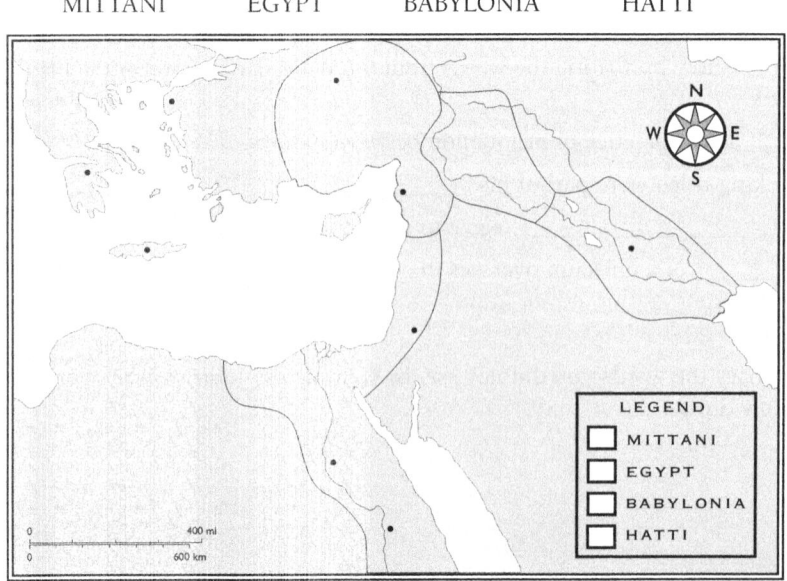

SUN WORSHIPPING: THE AMARNA PERIOD

CHAPTER SUMMARY

Amenhotep IV became king when his older brother unexpectedly died. Amenhotep IV changed his name to Akhenaten and decreed that Egyptians must abandon their gods and worship only one god.

ACCESS

Amenhotep IV was a young man who had strong personal ideas and may have had unusual physical characteristics as well. After you read the chapter, use the main idea map graphic organizer on page 8 of this study guide to help you more fully understand Amenhotep IV. In the large circle, write *Amenhotep IV*. In the surrounding circles, write details from the chapter about what Amenhotep IV may have looked like, how he felt about his family, and the changes he brought to Egypt.

CAST OF CHARACTERS

Write a complete sentence about each character.

Akhenaten (ahk-ken-NAH-ton) _____

_____

Nefertiti (nef-er-TEE-tee) _____

_____

WHAT HAPPENED WHEN?

In a complete sentence, tell what happened on the following dates:

1350–1334 BCE _____

750 BCE _____

The mid-1300s BCE in Egypt was known as "The Golden Age." In several complete sentences, explain why.

_____

_____

_____

WORD BANK

proverb   grouse   embalmers   monotheist

Complete the sentences below by writing the words from the Word Bank in the blanks. One word is not used.

_____ prepare a body for burial.

A person who believes in only one god is a _____.

A _____ is a saying that is believed to be generally true or wise.

WITH A PARENT OR PARTNER

The prefix *mono* comes from the Greek word *monos* and means "one." In five minutes, write all the words you can think of that start with *mono*. Ask a parent or partner to do the same. Then read your lists to each other. Look up in a dictionary any words either of you don't know.

CRITICAL THINKING

COMPARE AND CONTRAST

Thebes and Memphis were very different kinds of cities that served different cultural purposes. Read the chapter and then enter the following descriptive words and phrases about Memphis and Thebes in the appropriate column of the chart.

scribes	government	northern capital	governors
temples	columns	archives	secret rituals
business	documents	Amen	southern capital
priests	gods		

MEMPHIS	THEBES

COMPREHENSION

In the Cast of Characters section at the front of your book, Amenhotep IV (Akhenaten) is described as a "heretic king of Egypt." Judging from what you have learned about Amenhotep, write a definition of *heretic* in your history journal. Then look the word up in your dictionary to check your definition. Write a short paragraph telling why Amenhotep was a heretic.

WORKING WITH PRIMARY SOURCES

Proverbs are sayings that are used to teach wisdom and truth. One of the proverbs that Amenhotep IV would have been familiar with was *Report a thing observed, not heard.* Copy this proverb in your history journal. Then answer these questions:

- What do you think the proverb means?
- What is wise or true about it?

After you have answered the questions, write a paragraph in your history journal that rephrases the proverb in your own words. Explain why this proverb might be important (or no longer important) in the world today.

CHAPTER 16

ONLY TOMB WILL TELL: TUTANKHAMEN

CHAPTER SUMMARY

In 1922, Howard Carter discovered the tomb of Tutankhamen, the king who was probably the son of Akhenaten. The tomb was full of treasures and artifacts and took years to excavate fully.

ACCESS

WHAT DO YOU KNOW?

Perhaps you have heard of King Tut. How much do you already know about him? Use the K-W-L graphic organizer on page 8 of this study guide to begin to understand more about Tutankhamen and the discovery of his tomb. In the *What I Know* column, write everything you already know on the subject. Fill in the *What I Want to Know* column with questions, and as you read the chapter, write the answers to your questions and other interesting facts about Tutankhamen and his tomb in the *What I Learned* column.

CAST OF CHARACTERS

Write a complete sentence to explain why each character was significant.

Howard Carter _____

_____

Tutankhamen (toot-an-KAH-mun) _____

_____

Maya _____

_____

Horemheb _____

_____

Ay _____

_____

WHAT HAPPENED WHEN?

TIMELINE

Using the timeline graphic organizer on page 9 of this study guide, arrange the following dates in Howard Carter's diary from 1922 chronologically from top to bottom, then briefly describe what happened on each date in the corresponding boxes.

> November 5
>
> November 24
>
> November 26
>
> November 27

WORD BANK

sarcophagus   tomb   embalmers

Choose a word from the Word Bank to complete the sentence below.

A _____ is a stone coffin.

WORD PLAY

In the 1920s there was less scientific understanding of what we might learn from certain types of artifacts. Because of this lack of understanding, some of the items discovered in the tomb of Tutankhamen were damaged or destroyed, and their information was lost forever. Today, a variety of scientists would be sent to very carefully study clues at an Egyptian excavation site. Look up the words below in the dictionary and write a complete sentence about how each of these sciences might be used at a tomb excavation.

botany   radiology

_____

_____

_____

CRITICAL THINKING
OUTLINE

The excavation of Tutankhamen's tomb was both a frustrating and an exciting process for Howard Carter and his workers because the work proceeded so slowly but such amazing discoveries were made. In your history journal, copy the outline graphic organizer on page 8 of this study guide to help you more fully understand the process of excavating Tutankhamen's tomb. Create your outline with three "main idea" lines, then fill in several details from the chapter beneath each of the following topics.

Main Idea I: Excavating the passageways and doorways

Main Idea II: What was found in the antechamber

Main Idea III: What was found in Tutankhamen's burial chamber

COMPREHENSION

After reading the chapter, answer the following questions about Tutankhamen, the excavation of his tomb, and the study of mummified bodies in complete sentences in your history journal.

1. How old was Tutankhamen when he became king?

2. How old was Tutankhamen when he died?

3. Was he a large person?

4. Why did Tutankhamen change his name from Tutankhaten?

5. Why was Tutankhamen's innermost coffin so heavy?

6. Why was his body stuck to his coffin?

7. What modern technology can we use to tell us what a mummified person's face might have looked like?

8. What animals were the symbols of Upper and Lower Egypt? Where were these symbols found on Tutankhamen's human-shaped coffin?

READ MORE

To learn more about Howard Carter and Tutankhamen, see the Further Reading suggestions at the end of *The Ancient Egyptian World*.

SURVIVING CHILDHOOD: GROWING UP IN ANCIENT EGYPT

CHAPTER SUMMARY

Children in ancient Egypt were generally valued. Many children enjoyed toys and pets, and privileged boys went to school. Dreadful diseases took the lives of many young Egyptians, and parents tried medicine and magic to protect their children.

ACCESS

The lives of Egyptian children were similar in many ways to children's lives today, but there were many differences. As you read this chapter, list the details of the daily lives of Egyptian children in the chart below. Note details about toys and play, pets, and education. Then list details of how kids play today, what pets they have, and what their education is like. Highlight similarities between the two columns in one color and differences in another color.

ANCIENT EGYPTIAN CHILDREN	MODERN AMERICAN CHILDREN

BUILDING BACKGROUND

How did the Egyptians feel about babies? What kind of parents were they? In your history journal create a main idea map graphic organizer (see page 8 of this study guide) to answer these questions. In three large central circles, write *Pregnancy, Childbirth*, and *Babies*. In circles surrounding the central ideas, write facts about each subject that you learn as you read the chapter.

WORD BANK

amulets   ibis   apprentice   spell

Use words from the Word Bank to fill in the blanks in the following sentences. One word is not used at all.

An _____ is a bird that wades in water and has a long, curved bill.

Egyptians wore charms known as _____ to protect them against disease or evil.

An _____ learns a craft or a trade by doing the work with the help and teaching of a skilled worker.

WORD PLAY

If necessary, look up in a dictionary the word you did not use. Then write a sentence using that word that shows the word's meaning.

_____

WITH A PARENT OR PARTNER

The Egyptian word for cat was *myw*, which is similar to the English word for the sound that cats make (*meow*). "Meow" is an example of *onomatopoeia* (*ah-no-mah-toh-PEE-uh*). These are words that name a thing or an action by imitating its sound. Another example of onomatopoeia is "buzz." With a parent or a friend, read the following clues and fill in the blanks with the correct onomatopoeia words.

1. The sound of a leaky faucet: _____

2. The sound of a basketball going through a net: _____

3. The sound of a car engine: _____

4. The sound a dog makes: _____

5. The sound of a car horn: _____

6. The sound of bells: _____

7. The sound of thunder: _____

COMPREHENSION

We have learned much about ancient Egyptian life from the body of the peasant boy Nakht. After you read the chapter, answer the following questions about Nakht.

1. Why is the body of Nakht so valuable to us?

_____

_____

2. What diseases did Nakht suffer from?

_____

_____

3. How did Egyptian parents try to combat or prevent such illnesses as Nakht suffered?

_____

_____

WRITE ABOUT IT

Ancient Egyptians were very fond of cats. What do you think the life of a typical household cat might have been like? Review the information on page 126. Then imagine that you are a cat living in an ancient Egyptian household. In your history journal, write a short biographical essay about yourself. What did you look like? What were you fed, and how did you spend your day? Where did you sleep? How did people treat you?

18 WAR AND PEACE: RAMESSES II AND THE BATTLE OF QADESH

CHAPTER SUMMARY

Ramesses II led the Egyptian army against the Hittites, who controlled an important trade route. The actual outcome of the battle is in doubt, but it resulted in a peace agreement that was the earliest written treaty.

ACCESS

BUILDING BACKGROUND

We know a fair amount about Ramesses II from ancient Egyptian art, architecture, and written history. Before you read the chapter, read the sidebars about Ramesses II on pages 129, 130, and 131. In your history journal, copy the main idea map graphic organizer from page 8 of this study guide to help you more fully understand Ramesses II. In the central circle, write *Ramesses II*. In the surrounding circles, write words and phrases from the sidebars that describe what we know about him.

CAST OF CHARACTERS

Write a complete sentence about each character.

Ramesses II (RAM-ah-seas) _____

_____

Nefertari _____

_____

Menna _____

_____

WHAT HAPPENED WHEN?

In complete sentences, tell what happened in the following years of Ramesses II's rule. Then answer the questions.

Year 5 _____

Year 21 _____

During which dynasty did Ramesses II rule? _____

During which century BCE did this dynasty's rule begin? _____

WORD BANK

regnal   allegiance   division   rendezvous   fraternity   treaty

Complete the sentences below by writing the words from the Word Bank in the blanks. Two words are not used.

A large group of soldiers is called a _____.

_____ between the king of Egypt and the Hittite king means that they were like brothers.

A _____ is an agreement negotiated between nations.

_____ refers to the years of a king's reign.

WORD PLAY

Look up in a dictionary the two words not used, and write a complete sentence using each word in your history journal.

CRITICAL THINKING
CAUSE AND EFFECT

In Year 5 of his reign, Ramesses II led his army on a mission to regain control of the city-state of Qadesh from the Hittites. In your history journal create a T-chart graphic organizer similar to the one on page 9 of this study guide. Below is a list of events that occurred before and during the battle between the Egyptians and the Hittites. Write them in the order that they happened, matching causes with effects in the columns of your graphic organizer.

CAUSE	EFFECT
The Army of Re did not know that they were vulnerable and in mortal danger.	The Egyptians found two Hittite deserters hiding in the Wood of Labwi.
The Hittite deserters told Ramesses that the Hittite king was too frightened of Ramesses to proceed further.	The Army of Re soldiers panicked and scattered.
The Army of Re fled the battlefield.	Ramesses believed the deserters and took one division of the army toward Qadesh.
The Egyptian army stopped to rest in the Wood of Labwi and set up camp.	The Army of Re led the Hittite army directly toward Ramesses and the Army of Amen.
The Egyptian patrol captured two Hittite spies who told them that the Hittite king and army were just over the hill.	The Army of Re marched into a trap.
Hittite charioteers charged the Army of Re.	Ramesses knew that he had been tricked.

WORKING WITH PRIMARY SOURCES
COMPREHENSION

Royal Inscriptions, Qadesh Battle Inscriptions of Ramesses II (about 1279–1212 BCE)

Read the inscription on page 132 that describes Ramesses' heroic defeat of the Hittite army. In your history journal, answer the following questions in complete sentences, explaining your answers.

1. How likely is it that this story of Ramesses' heroism is true?

2. Why do you think the royal scribes wrote this story?

ALL OVER THE MAP
INTERACTION

1. Label the following cities, countries, and physical features on the map below.

Tigris River	Red Sea	Mediterranean Sea
Qadesh	Mesopotamia	Canaan
Amarna	Cyprus	Orontes River
Nile River	Hattusa	Euphrates River

2. Use shading or a pattern to indicate the territories of Egypt and Hatti. Then key these patterns in the legend.

3. The chapter states that whoever controlled the city-state of Qadesh controlled the trade route from the coast. Study Qadesh's location on the map, noting its position near bodies of water. In your history journal explain why Qadesh was so important.

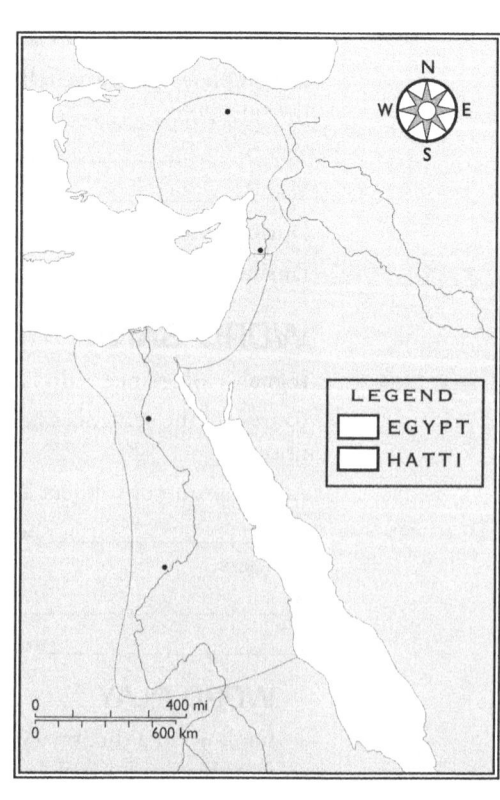

LEGEND
☐ EGYPT
☐ HATTI

SCRATCH AND SNIFF: VILLAGE LIFE

CHAPTER SUMMARY

Living conditions for the average villager in ancient Egypt were primitive. Houses were made of mud bricks, which would disintegrate in a short time. Water was scarce and was severely rationed.

ACCESS

If you were to explain to someone how you live, what would you talk about? You might describe your home, your family, the sights of your city, what you eat, your activities, and what people do to make a living. List these categories in a chart in your history journal. As you read about village life in ancient Egypt, jot down details about how ancient Egyptians lived.

WORD BANK

necropolis   incense   tell   floodplain

Complete the sentences below by writing words from the Word Bank in the blanks. One word is not used.

You can hide a bad odor by burning _____.

_____ is a Greek word that means "city of the dead."

Archaeologists can learn details about past settlements by excavating a _____.

WORD PLAY

Write a sentence using the word you did not use, clearly showing that word's meaning.

_____

CRITICAL THINKING

After you read the chapter, put a checkmark beside any of the following features you might expect to find in an ancient Egyptian house.

____ mud bricks	____ basement	____ bathroom	____ entrance hall
____ fleas	____ garage	____ red door	____ couch
____ brick oven	____ windows	____ cloth door	____ onions
____ bed	____ candles	____ ice	____ fireplace
____ books	____ sack of beans	____ people sleeping on roof	

In your history journal, draw a blueprint, or map, of a typical ancient Egyptian house based on the general layout descriptions on pages 131–138. Label the rooms and features of the house on your blueprint.

COMPREHENSION

Answer the following questions in complete sentences in your history journal.

1. Why did the Egyptians burn incense in their homes?

2. Why were the houses at Deir el-Medina somewhat nicer than the houses in other villages?

3. What is a barter system?

4. Why was it a punishment to be sent to the back of the house?

DO THE MATH

The chapter tells us that at Deir el-Medina an average six-person household would be given about four gallons of water per person, per day, for drinking and bathing. Based on this estimate, answer the following questions:

1. How many total gallons of water per day would a household of eight people be given? _____

2. How many total gallons per "week" (ten Egyptian workdays) would the same family of eight receive? _____

WORKING WITH PRIMARY SOURCES

Notes on ostraca (broken pots) found at Deir el-Medina, about 1293–1070 BCE

- "I am wretched; I am searching for my sight but it is gone."

- "Since I was a child until today, I have been with you."

- "Seek out for me one tunic in exchange for the ring; I will allow you ten days."

- "I will do it! See, I will do it, I will do it!"

WRITE ABOUT IT

The inscribed fragments of ostraca found at Deir el-Medina are like pieces of torn-up personal letters; their partial messages tantalize us with their hidden stories. When you read the fragments of messages above, do you wonder who these people were, and what their circumstances might have been? Were they happy in their lives, or struggling? Choose one of the messages above, and on a page in your history journal write a biographical sketch of the person you imagine might have written it. Describe the following details about this person:

- name
- age
- male or female
- what the person looks like
- what is happening or has happened to the person and how the person feels about it
- who the person is writing to, and why
- why the person used these particular words

READ MORE

To learn more about village life, see the Further Reading suggestions at the end of *The Ancient Egyptian World*.

BATTLE STATIONS: THE SEA PEOPLES

CHAPTER SUMMARY

During the reign of Ramesses III, the feared Sea Peoples threatened to invade Egypt. Using superior military strategy and a highly trained army, Ramesses III defeated the Sea Peoples and saved Egypt from destruction.

ACCESS

The chapter tells us that the mysterious Sea Peoples changed the ancient world dramatically. How do you think this was so? After you read the chapter, use the main idea map graphic organizer on page 8 of this study guide to organize our knowledge about the Sea Peoples. In the central circle, write *Sea Peoples*. In the surrounding circles, write words and phrases from the chapter that describe what we know about them and questions that we have about them.

CAST OF CHARACTERS

Write a complete sentence describing Ramesses (RAM-ah-seas) III.

_____

WHAT HAPPENED WHEN?

According to the chapter, what was happening in the eastern Mediterranean region in the late

13th century BCE? _____

_____

WORD BANK

mortuary   galley   javelin   maneuver

Complete the sentences below by writing in the blanks the words from the Word Bank. One word is not used.

The Sea Peoples used a spearlike weapon known as a _____.

A _____ is a military movement made to gain an advantage over the enemy.

The word _____ has to do with death or the burial of the dead.

WORD PLAY

The prefix *mort* in the word *mortuary* comes from Latin and means "death." Another word with the prefix *mort* is *mortal*, which has several possible meanings. Look up *mortal* in a dictionary and write two of its definitions in your history journal. Write original sentences using *mortal* with each of these meanings.

CRITICAL THINKING
COMPARE AND CONTRAST

Compare and contrast the armies of the Egyptians and the Sea Peoples. Draw a large two-circle Venn diagram in your history journal (see page 9 of this study guide). Label one circle *Sea Peoples* and the other *Egyptians*. Write the details from the chapter listed below in the appropriate circles. Write any shared details in the overlapping area.

- used archers
- disorderly and chaotic
- used grappling hooks
- boats with oars
- charioteers
- orderly rows
- conquered the Hittites
- boats with sails
- swords and spears
- homeless
- could lose their homeland

COMPREHENSION
OUTLINE

Ramesses III's victory against the Sea Peoples is the main theme of the art and architecture of his mortuary temple. Use the outline graphic organizer on page 8 of this study guide to help you more fully understand this important event in ancient Egyptian history. Draw an outline in your history journal with the four main ideas listed below. Write several details from the chapter beneath each of the topics.

Topic I: Who the Sea Peoples were and why they were attacking Egypt

Topic II: What Ramesses III did to try to stop the Sea Peoples

Topic III: The defeat of the Sea Peoples' army

Topic IV: The defeat of the Sea Peoples' navy

WRITE ABOUT IT

In complete sentences in your history journal, describe the crucial advantages the Egyptians had that allowed them to conquer the Sea Peoples in the Nile delta.

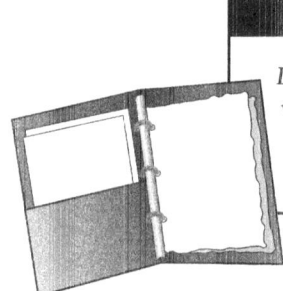

HISTORY JOURNAL

Don't forget to share your history journal with your classmates, and ask if you can see what their journals look like. You might be surprised—and get some new ideas.

HAPPILY EVER AFTER: THE ARTS

CHAPTER SUMMARY

Ancient Egyptian artists followed very specific style rules. Egyptians believed that art had magical properties. They discovered and used the "sacred ratio" in their art and architecture. Many stories that are familiar to us today may have begun in Egyptian literature.

ACCESS

BUILDING BACKGROUND

The opening pages of the chapter give us several important details about ancient Egyptian art. To begin exploring this subject, read the first three paragraphs of the chapter and then answer these questions in your history journal in complete sentences.

Paragraph 1

1. What were three rules that ancient Egyptians followed in drawing or sculpture?

Paragraph 2

2. What is frontalism?

3. How long did the use of frontalism last?

4. Why was it important to Egyptians to show many parts of the body?

Paragraph 3

5. What did the "scribes of outlines" do?

6. What did "colorists" do?

CAST OF CHARACTERS

According to the Cast of Characters on page 11, who was Strabo (STRAY-bow)?

_____

What other well-known tale is the fictional story of Rhodopis like?

_____

WORD BANK

innovator   sacred ratio   percussion

Complete the sentences below with words from the Word Bank. One word is not used.

The _____ is a precise proportion of length to width.

Someone who is an _____ might break the rules of style.

WORD PLAY

Write a sentence that shows the meaning of the word you did not use.

_____

CRITICAL THINKING
COMPARE AND CONTRAST

The ancient Egyptians discovered and used the measurements known as the "sacred ratio" in most of their art and architecture. The chapter tells us that the sacred ratio is found throughout the universe and that the Egyptians applied it to many of their creations. Use the main idea map on page 8 of this study guide to explore this idea. In your history journal write *The Sacred Ratio* at the top of a page. Then draw two large circles, labeling one *Nature* and the other *Egyptian Art*. In smaller connecting circles write the following items from art and nature where appropriate.

- jewelry
- nautilus shell spiral
- tombs
- galaxies
- hieroglyphs
- temples
- sunflowers
- pyramids
- pinecones
- human body

MAKING INFERENCES

Why do you think that ancient Egyptians called this measurement that is found throughout the universe "sacred"? Write your answer in complete sentences in your history journal.

WORKING WITH PRIMARY SOURCES

Egyptian story of Cinderella retold by Strabo (about 63 BCE–21 CE)

You probably recognize the plot of the story of Rhodopis. Use the sequence of events graphic organizer on page 9 of this study guide to put the events of the story listed below in the correct order from beginning to end.

- The old man bought beautiful shoes for Rhodopis.
- The king searched for the woman who could wear the beautiful shoe.
- Rhodopis had too many chores to go to the king's party.
- Rhodopis was kidnapped and sold to a kind old Egyptian.
- The shoe fit Rhodopis, and she pulled the other one from her tunic.
- They lived happily ever after.
- Horus, disguised as a falcon, snatched one of the shoes from Rhodopis and flew away.
- Horus dropped the shoe in the king's lap.
- The other servants were mean to Rhodopis.

COMPREHENSION

Music was very important to the ancient Egyptians. After reading the chapter, answer the following questions.

1. How do we know that ancient Egyptians enjoyed music?

_____

_____

2. What kinds of instruments did they use?

_____

_____

WRITE ABOUT IT

Is music important to you? If so, why? What kinds of music do you enjoy? In your history journal, write a paragraph that tells how you feel about music.

KING FOR A DAY: KUSH, NUBIA, AND THE THIRD INTERMEDIATE PERIOD

CHAPTER SUMMARY

During the Third Intermediate Period, Egypt was weak and fractured into competing states. Finally, King Piye of Kush, a kingdom to the south, brought an army into Egypt and reunited the Two Lands. From that time on, Egypt was ruled by foreign dynasties.

ACCESS

What do you know about King Piye and Kush? What would you like to know? Use the K-W-L graphic organizer on page 8 of this study guide to explore these subjects. In the *What I Know* column, write everything you already know on the subject. Fill in the *What I Want to Know* column with your questions, and as you read the chapter write the answers to your questions and other interesting facts in the *What I Learned* column.

CAST OF CHARACTERS

Write a complete sentence describing the significance of each of these characters.

Strabo (STRAY-bow) _____

Piye (PEE-yee) _____

What other name was Piye known by? _____

WHAT HAPPENED WHEN?

In complete sentences, write what happened on the following dates.

about 747–716 BCE _____

about 20 CE _____

WORD BANK

nomadic   ambassador   contempt   obligation

Choose words from the word bank to complete the sentences. One word is not used.

An _____ is the diplomatic representative of a foreign government.

The King of Dor treated Wenamun with _____, or a lack of respect.

Another word for *duty* is _____.

WORD PLAY

Look up in a dictionary the word that you did not use. Write that word in a sentence.

_____

CRITICAL THINKING
CAUSE AND EFFECT

In the Third Intermediate Period, a weakened Egypt was in chaos until King Piye reunited the Two Lands. Read the chapter, and in your history journal create a T-chart graphic organizer similar to the one on page 9 of this study guide. On the next page is a list of causes and effects that occurred during the time of King Piye. Write them in the order that they happened, matching causes with effects in the columns of your graphic organizer. Then answer the questions.

CAUSE	EFFECT
Kush's archers were very skilled.	It became a wealthy and strong country.
King Piye appointed his sister "the Divine Wife of the God."	It lost respect in the ancient world.
Kush had gold mines.	The Egyptians called it *Ta-Seti*, "The Land of the Bow."
The priests at Thebes became very powerful.	She became ruler of Upper Egypt.
Egypt became fractured and disorganized.	The pharaoh's power was weakened.

WITH A PARENT OR PARTNER

When you've finished your chart, read aloud the sentences to a parent or partner, connecting each cause to each effect with the word *so*.

COMPREHENSION

1. What is the Greek word for *Nubia*, and what is its English translation?

_____

2. How did someone become a priest during the Third Intermediate Period?

_____

3. List some of the foreign groups that conquered Egypt during the Third Intermediate Period.

_____

4. What does the name that Piye took, *Sema-tawy*, mean?

_____

WRITE ABOUT IT

Read the last two paragraphs of the chapter, which describe King Piye. We are told that he was a "compassionate" man. What other words might describe Piye? In your history journal, write two other adjectives that you believe describe Piye, as a king, a military leader, or a human being. Explain your word choices in complete sentences.

ALL OVER THE MAP

Study the map below and then do the following exercises.

1. Label the following cities, countries, and geographic features.

   Kush   Dor   Red Sea   Nubia

   Mediterranean Sea   Nile River

   Upper Egypt   Canaan   Thebes

   Lower Egypt   Egypt

2. Read the story of the priest Wenamun on pages 150–152. Then trace his journey from Thebes to Dor on the map.

3. How far did Wenamun travel to get from Karnak, in Thebes, to Dor? Use the mileage scale to calculate your answer.

_____

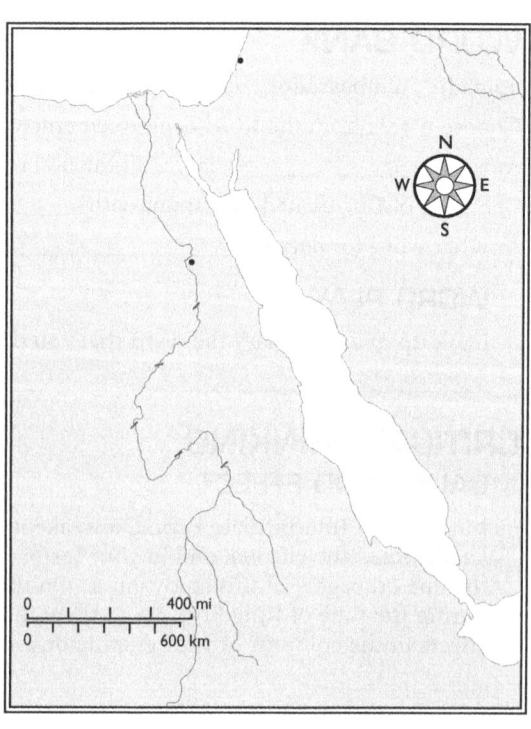

GREAT EXPECTATIONS: THE GREEK PERIOD

CHAPTER SUMMARY

The Egyptians of the 4th century BCE, who had suffered religious and economic persecution under Persian rule, welcomed the Macedonian leader Alexander the Great. Alexander was a bold conqueror who founded the city of Alexandria.

ACCESS

Have you ever heard of Alexander the Great? Who was he, and what was so great about him? In your history journal, copy the K-W-L graphic organizer on page 8 of this study guide to help you learn more about Alexander and his conquest of Egypt. In the *What I Know* column, write everything you already know on the subject. Fill in the *What I Want to Know* column with your questions, and as you read the chapter write the answers to your questions and other interesting facts in the *What I Learned* column.

CAST OF CHARACTERS

Write a complete sentence describing the significance of each of these characters.

Alexander the Great _____

_____

Aristotle _____

_____

Plutarch (PLOO-tark)_____

_____

Arrian _____

_____

THINK ABOUT IT

What are the titles of the two famous long poems written by Homer?

_____

WHAT HAPPENED WHEN?

In your history journal, copy the timeline graphic organizer on page 9 of this study guide. Then arrange the following dates relating to Alexander's conquest of Egypt in chronological order from top to bottom. Briefly describe what happened on each date in the corresponding boxes.

April 331 BCE

336 BCE

November 14, 332 BCE

late October 332 BCE

WORD BANK

invincible   descendant   tribute   odyssey   oasis

Choose words from the Word Bank to complete the sentences. Two of the words are not used.

An _____ is a long, wandering journey.

A service or a gift given to show respect is a _____.

Someone who cannot be overcome or conquered is _____.

WORD PLAY

Look up in a dictionary the words that you did not use, and write each word in a sentence in your history journal.

CRITICAL THINKING

OUTLINE

Alexander the Great was a very religious person, and religion played a large part in his successful conquest of Egypt. In your history journal, make an outline modeled after the outline graphic organizer on page 8 of this study guide to explore this idea. Write the following topics in four main idea lines:

Topic I: Egyptian life and religion under Persian rule

Topic II: Alexander's first impressions of Egypt and its religion

Topic III: How Alexander practiced religion while living in Egypt

Topic IV: How the Egyptians felt about Alexander

Then write several details from pages 157–159 beneath each of these main ideas.

WORKING WITH PRIMARY SOURCES

Plutarch, *Life of Alexander* (about 79 CE)

> At the end of the story of young Alexander's wise and brave handling of the wild stallion, Alexander's father the king says to him, "Seek another kingdom, my son, that may be worthy of your abilities; for Macedonia is too small for you."

What does the king mean when he says that Macedonia is "too small" for Alexander? How does he feel about his son's future? In your history journal, write a paragraph that answers these questions. Be sure to explain your answers.

WITH A PARENT OR PARTNER

Alexander's favorite hero was the warrior Achilles, from Homer's poem the *Iliad*. What do we mean when we say someone has an "Achilles' heel"? How did this phrase come about? With a parent or an older family member, do an Internet search using the phrase "Achilles' heel mythology." Describe your findings about the origin and meaning of "Achilles' heel" in your history journal.

READ MORE

To learn more about Alexander the Great and his conquest of Egypt, see the Further Reading suggestions at the end of *The Ancient Egyptian World*.

THE LAST CHAPTER: GRAECO-ROMAN RULE

CHAPTER SUMMARY

The centuries of Graeco-Roman rule in Egypt were a time of intense political drama and great intellectual and scientific achievement.

ACCESS

BUILDING BACKGROUND

This chapter describes several fascinating political leaders of the Graeco-Roman rule over Egypt, including Cleopatra VII. She was an intelligent and creative politician with a strong sense of drama. In your history journal, copy the main idea map graphic organizer from page 8 of this study guide to help you better understand Cleopatra's life. In the central circle, write *Cleopatra VII*. In the surrounding circles, write words and phrases from the chapter that describe her personal qualities and abilities, her cultural achievements, and the methods she used to influence rulers and statesmen.

CAST OF CHARACTERS

The final period of ancient Egyptian history features a cast of unforgettable and vivid personalities. In your history journal, make a list of the following characters. As you read the chapter, next to each name write a brief phrase that describes why he or she is historically significant.

General Ptolemy (TALL-uh-mee)	Cleopatra VII
Ptolemy III	Julius Caesar
Eratosthenes	Mark Antony
Pliny the Elder	Archimedes
Sostrates (SAUCE-trah-tees)	Euclid
Ptolemy II	Heron
Ptolemy XII	Ptolemy (astronomer, geographer)
Berenice	Aristarcus of Samos

WHAT HAPPENED WHEN?

TIMELINE

By now you know something about all the major time periods of the ancient Egyptian world. Use the timeline graphic organizer on page 9 of this study guide as a model for creating a final timeline in your history journal. Include all the periods you have studied, listed below, in the correct chronological order, from earliest to last.

New Kingdom Period (1570–1070 BCE)

First Intermediate Period (2181–2040 BCE)

Late Period (525–332 BCE)

Early Dynastic Period (3050–2686 BCE)

Hellenistic (Greek) Period (332–30 BCE)

Third Intermediate Period (1069–525 BCE)

Middle Kingdom Period (2040–1782 BCE)

Graeco-Roman Period (305–30 BCE)

Old Kingdom Period (2686–2184 BCE)

Second Intermediate Period (1782–1570 BCE)

DO THE MATH

How many years passed between the beginnings of ancient Egypt in the Early Dynastic Period (3050 BCE) and the end of Egypt as an independent state (30 BCE)?

WORD BANK

parchment   ambition   opulence   stellar

Choose words from the Word Bank to complete the following sentences.

The word _____ comes from the Latin word meaning "star."

_____, made from untanned animal skins, was more flexible and durable than papyrus.

The _____, or wealth, of Cleopatra's court was displayed dramatically to Julius Caesar and Mark Antony.

_____ is the desire to achieve a particular goal.

WORD PLAY

The Museum in Alexandria was dedicated to the Muses, who were the Greek goddesses of arts and science. What does the verb *muse* mean? Look it up in your dictionary, and write the definition in your history journal. Then use the word *muse* in a complete sentence.

CRITICAL THINKING

The discoveries made and the ideas developed at the Museum in Alexandria laid the groundwork for our continuing scientific and artistic growth to the present day. In your history journal, make an outline to understand more fully the legacy of the Museum (refer to the outline graphic organizer on page 8 of this study guide). Write several details from the chapter beneath each of the following main ideas.

Topic I: The purpose of the Museum, and the subjects studied

Topic II: The life of scholars at the Museum

Topic III: Math, medicine, mechanics, and maps

IN YOUR OWN WORDS

The brilliant astronomer and geographer Ptolemy wrote,

> Well do I know that I am mortal, a creature of one day.
>
> But if my mind follows the winding paths of the stars
>
> Then my feet no longer rest on earth, but standing by
>
> Zeus himself I take my fill of ambrosia, the divine dish.

What do you think this passage means? What was Ptolemy saying about life? What did he want to do with his own life, and why? In your history journal, rewrite Ptolemy's thoughts in your own words, using his style of writing. Then add to them: What do I want to do with *my* life?

REPORTS AND SPECIAL PROJECTS

There's always more to find out about the ancient Egyptian world. Take a look at the Further Reading section at the end of the book (pages 176–181). Here you'll find a number of books on different topics relating to ancient Egypt. Many of them will be available in your school or local public library.

GETTING STARTED

Explore the Further Reading section for any of these reasons:

— You're curious and want to learn more about a particular topic.

— You want to do a research report on ancient Egypt.

— You still have questions about something covered in the book.

— You need more information for a special classroom project.

What's the best way to find the books that will help you the most?

LOOK AT THE SUBHEADS

The books are organized by topic. The subhead "Daily Life" tells you where to find books telling about the life of ancient Egyptians, for example. Go to "Mummies and Life After Death" to learn more about how Egyptians prepared for life after death. Let the subheads give you ideas for reports and special projects.

LOOK AT THE BOOK TITLES

The titles of the books can tell you a lot about what's inside. The books listed under "Cleopatra" will give you a good picture of how our understanding and perspective on the famous Egyptian queen have changed over the years.

LOOK FOR GENERAL REFERENCES

This section also lists general books, which are useful starting points for further research. "General Works on Ancient Egypt" will list titles that provide a broad overview of the ancient Egyptian experience. Judge by the titles which books will be the most useful to you. Other references include:

• Dictionaries

• Encyclopedias

• Atlases

OTHER RESOURCES

Information comes in all kinds of formats. Use the book to learn about primary sources. Go to the library for videos, DVDs, and audio materials. And don't forget about the Internet!

AUDIO-VISUAL MATERIALS

Your school or local library can offer documentary videos and DVDs on early humankind, as well as audio materials. If you have access to a computer, explore the sites listed on the section titled Websites (pages 182–183) for some good jumping-off points. These are organized by topic, with brief descriptions of what you'll find on the site. Many websites list additional reading, as well as other Internet links you can visit.

What you've learned about the ancient Egyptian world so far is just a beginning. Learning more is an ongoing adventure!

LIBRARY / MEDIA CENTER RESEARCH LOG

NAME _____

DUE DATE _____

What I Need to **Find**

I need to use:

☐ primary
☐ secondary

[ ] sources.

Places I **Know** to Look

Brainstorm: Other Sources and Places to Look

Rate each source from 1 (low) to 4 (high) in the categories below

helpful

relevant

WHAT I FOUND

How I Found it

Suggestion
Library Catalog
Browsing
Internet Search
Web link

Primary Source
Secondary Source

Book/Periodical
Website
Other

<u>Title/Author/Location (call # or URL)</u>

Lightning Source UK Ltd.
Milton Keynes UK
UKOW06f0323060215

245744UK00001B/36/P